Reflections II: The Lifetouch Family Album

LIFETOUCH INC.

© 1994 by Lifetouch Inc. All rights reserved.

Lifetouch Inc.
7831 Glenroy Road
Minneapolis, MN 55439

Library of Congress Catalog Number:
94-077 256

ISBN: 0-9617259-0-7

Printed in the United States of America

Produced by Mundale Communications
Editor and Project Director: Susan Mundale

Research & Writing: Mame Osteen

Design & Art Direction: Rachel Fine

Typography: Anne Shannon, P&H Photo Composition

Printing: Diversified Graphics, Inc.,
        Minneapolis, Minnesota

Photo Credits:

The Bettmann Archive: p. 42, Statue of Liberty; p. 51, Margaret Thatcher; p. 71, U.S. Hockey Team, Prince Charles and Lady Diana Spencer, Americans held hostage; p. 77, Madonna, Chernobyl power plant; p. 97, New York Stock Exchange, Berlin Wall; p. 109, Desert Storm, Children of Sarajevo, Nelson Mandela.

Minnesota Historical Society: p. 13, Franklin D. Roosevelt, Find Your War Job Poster; p. 33, Rock and Rollers, Elvis Presley fans, President Kennedy; p. 43, The Beatles, War Protest; p. 51, Minnesota Twins postcard.

Star Tribune: p. 51, Jimmy Carter.

CONTENTS

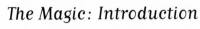

FOREWORD

*I*n 1986, we published Reflections: The Lifetouch Family Album *to celebrate the growth of the Lifetouch family through our first half century in business. In the eight years since our 50th anniversary, Lifetouch has become a significantly different company. New technologies have changed our production processes dramatically. We have expanded our publishing capabilities and opened a second publishing operation in Love's Park, Illinois. We have added production facilities in Tulsa, Oklahoma, Chesapeake, Virginia, and Chico, California. We have continued to expand our reach into new territories throughout the United States, and into Canada and Mexico. We also continue to expand our product lines to reflect the changing marketplace.*

The number of people at Lifetouch has more than doubled in eight years—from 4,000 in 1986 to over 10,000 in 1994. This increase has come about through business growth and through acquisition of other companies in our field. Those new members of the Lifetouch family add greatly to our strength in the marketplace and the richness of our culture.

The texture of our company has changed as well. In the mid-1980s, we were just beginning to reflect the diversity of our marketplace in our sales force and production facilities; in 1994, we know that diversity is critical to our leadership in this industry.

Despite these changes, the values that sustained Lifetouch for its first half century have not changed. We still believe in the importance of family—the Lifetouch family, the families of our people, and the families of our customers. We still believe in providing our customers with the highest quality product possible and with service that builds long-term relationships. We are more convinced than ever that employee ownership is a solid foundation for the future of our company.

As with any family, it is important for Lifetouch to remember and acknowledge its roots. We are thankful to Eldon Rothgeb and Bruce Reinecker for the company they created. By publishing this book, Reflections II, we add the events of the past eight years to the Lifetouch story, and direct our company forward into the twenty-first century.

Richard P. Erickson
Chairman and Chief Executive Officer
July 1, 1994

Paul Harmel
President and Chief Operating Officer
July 1, 1994

Eldon S. Rothgeb

THE *Magic*

Lifetouch is a company that directly touches the lives of many people. A recognized leader in school and portrait photography, Lifetouch has been capturing the memories of millions of families and individuals for nearly 60 years.

The Lifetouch story began in 1936, when Bruce Reinecker and Eldon Rothgeb made plans to bring their "School Photography of Distinction" to one-room schoolhouses throughout rural Minnesota. Sharing a tiny apartment, a cramped office, and a dream, the two hopeful and ambitious young men poured their skills and talents into their company, National School Studios.

Eldon Rothgeb and Bruce Reinecker posed with NSS employees in the 1940s (above). A picture man operated NSS's early box camera (center). NSS employees mailed orders to schools (below). Rothgeb and Reinecker celebrated a golf victory in 1939 (left).

1

R. Bruce Runciman

Rothgeb, the master salesman, built a loyal, hardworking sales force that expanded the company's reach from coast to coast. Reinecker, the innovator, consistently championed new production technologies in an eternal quest for greater efficiency within the company and higher quality for the customer. Along the way, the partners' dream became reality. Little more than a decade after its founding, National School Studios was the largest school photography firm in the country.

But size alone doesn't make a great company. People do. And beginning with its founders, Lifetouch has been blessed with leaders whose loyalty and devotion to employees and customers have been paramount.

Hal Ridges used the job-ticket holder given to him in 1948 by Eldon Rothgeb. Employees gathered for the 1952 NSS sales meeting (center). Candy, Margaret, Helen, and Rosella celebrated Christmas in the 1950s (below, from left). NSS sunbathing beauties relaxed at a company picnic in 1952 (left).

When founder Eldon Rothgeb died in 1972, Bruce Reinecker was besieged with offers to buy his company. Instead, he looked within its ranks for new leadership that could take the company forward. And there he found Richard Erickson, a territory manager who had joined the company fresh from the U.S. Army in 1955.

In 1964, many NSS employees participated in the company bowling league (above). In 1961, Steve Subak, Eldon Rothgeb, and Bruce Reinecker (seated center) posed with the NSS salesforce "20-year men." The nation's bicentenial was the theme of the annual plant luncheon in 1976 (below). Micro-Z inventor Tal Hopson (below right) took a break with lens supplier Jan Terlouw in 1982.

For most employees, Chairman of the Board Richard Erickson embodies the heart and soul of the company. "Dick is the spiritual leader, the father of the Lifetouch family," said President and Chief Operating Officer Paul Harmel.

Richard Erickson (front row, fourth from left) and John Reid (right) attended a regional sales meeting in 1981. In 1980, Bruce Reinecker and longtime friends Fred Schaefer (left) and Joe Bianchi got together at the NSS summer sales meeting (below).

The "magic man," as he is often called, Erickson is the personification of the company's culture — a competitive risk-taker, a motivator, a strategic thinker. Yet he is also fun-loving, compassionate, and down-to-earth. Most of all, he has an abiding love for the company.

Erickson's vision brought Lifetouch from its entrepreneurial foundation to its position today — a multifaceted company with more than 10,000 employees during its peak periods every year. In the process, he has managed to maintain and pass on the qualities that brought Lifetouch the success it now enjoys — loyalty, respect, integrity, honesty. "Employees are the most important asset we have," said former vice president Bob Treuchel. "The people here come to realize that no matter who you are — whether you sweep the floors or are the president of the company — you are an important part of Lifetouch."

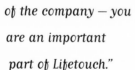

At Lifetouch, annual awards dinners are opportunities to celebrate individual achievement.

Founder Bruce
Reinecker demonstrated
his commitment to
Lifetouch people in 1978
when he created the
company's ESOP, which
transferred 100 percent
of the company's owner-
ship to employees. The
Employee Stock Ownership
Plan (ESOP) has provided many Lifetouch people
with financial rewards unimaginable in most
companies. The ESOP unites the Lifetouch family
with a sense of purpose. "It's something you
can't put your arms around and touch and
feel, but there's a magic there," said Treuchel.
"We're employee owned; we exist for each
other; our shareholders are ourselves.
We have a tremendous ob-
ligation to our customers,
and a tremendous respon-
sibility to our suppliers.
We represent a family."

Themes and costumes are a
Lifetouch party tradition. Hats
were the theme of a 1980
luncheon (above). Employees
turned the 1982 spring luncheon
into a hoe-down (center). Bruce
Reinecker with NSS employees
receiving 25-year awards at the
1983 service awards banquet.

The Lifetouch family extends beyond the workplace. After a challenging day at work, Lifetouch employees often get together for recreation and fun. And after completing a long career with the company, many Lifetouch retirees reunite two or three times a year at the annual sales meeting in Minneapolis and on tours and vacation trips sponsored by the company's Alumni Club. "It's a wonderful thing," said former Alumni Club president Fred Gowan. "It's a place to stay in touch with your friends."

Lifetouch retirees still get together at Alumni Club activities (above). In 1991, Alyce Hausam (left), Lil Darth (center), and Kathryn Lombard took the Alumni Club cruise to the Bahamas.

Lifetouch looks to a future built on the values that have made it strong in the past. "We need people with expertise, vitality, and broad vision," said Richard Erickson. "But they also need to have heart. That's what makes this organization go."

"We have three values at Lifetouch — people, integrity, and excellence," said Portrait Studios sales manager Ernie Denogeon. "We believe in our people, and we treat them fairly. We won't do business unless we can do it with integrity. And we strive for excellence in everything we do."

Where is Lifetouch headed? "We're on a fast train to success," said Denogeon. "We don't have time for stragglers."

The 50th Anniversary Committee clowned for the camera during preparations for the 1986 celebration. In 1992, Lifetouch Portrait Studios district managers received awards during their annual sales meeting.

THE SPARK

In 1936, Eldon Rothgeb and Bruce Reinecker launched National School Studios (NSS) — School Photography of Distinction — by raising $500 in start-up money and choosing Minnesota as their location. They rented a second-floor studio in downtown Minneapolis and got ready for the 1937-38 school year. During the next 35 years, with Rothgeb managing sales and Reinecker managing production, they built a nationwide company serving schools in 50 states. By 1972, NSS had become a $10 million enterprise and an industry leader in both products and production.

1936 to 1912

While America's leaders struggled to remedy the Great Depression and war brewed in Germany, two ambitious young salesmen with energy and an idea launched a school photography business in Minneapolis, Minnesota. They began in Roosevelt's New Deal and worked diligently through World War II, the postwar boom, and the Korean Conflict. Then, against a backdrop of the Cold War and the race for the moon, and through the civil rights movement, the war in Vietnam, and the social and political upheavals of the '60s and '70s, Eldon Rothgeb and Bruce Reinecker built National School Studios into a dynamic and innovative company, tops in its field.

1936 Franklin D. Roosevelt is reelected president in a landslide victory •

Rothgeb and Reinecker plan their school photography business, National School

Studios (NSS) **1938** U.S. establishes 40-hour work week • National School

Studios sales reach $65,000 **1939** Germany invades Poland, and

World War II begins • NSS introduces the 3″ x 5″ enlargement

1941 Japan bombs Pearl Harbor, U.S. enters the war **1942**

Bruce Reinecker, Carl Satre, and Steve Subak join the armed

services **1943** A diminished sales force and gas rationing cut NSS profits

1945 War in Europe ends; Japan surrenders

• NSS sales top $330,000.

"I've found the job where I fit best!"

FIND YOUR WAR JOB
In Industry – Agriculture – Business

The first NSS photos were black-and-white keepsakes.

By 1939, Reinecker (left) and Rothgeb had a thriving business.

Realizing A Dream: *1921-1949*

As a young man, Bruce Reinecker had a dream. "This is a great land of opportunity, and I intend to make the most of it," Bruce told his father, Joseph, a Kansas farmer whose own dreams had failed in the 1920s. "I expect to retire by the time I'm 30." To realize his dream, Reinecker became a salesman. He was a natural — tall, handsome, and ambitious. Sales jobs were plentiful in the 1920s, and even during the Great Depression sales offered opportunities for hard-working men willing to forego guaranteed wages for commissions. By 1934, Reinecker, a salesman for a meat-packing company, had been successful at a variety of jobs, but he was far from his boasted "retirement" — except in age.

The Picture Man

That year, Reinecker met Eldon ("Eldy") Rothgeb in a Kansas City cafeteria. Rothgeb was a stocky, sharp-witted dynamo with a head for business. Though his father was a University of Missouri School of Agriculture professor and a successful hog farmer, Rothgeb preferred photography to the farm. At 17, he had started work for McClellan Studios in Kansas City, driving the roads of Illinois with his camera and stopping at schools to take pictures of students.

Over dinner, Reinecker and Rothgeb talked about their jobs. While Reinecker found the meat-packing business merely "interesting," Rothgeb was ebullient about being a "picture man," where the opportunities were unlimited. Ten days later, Reinecker was selling school pictures in southern Minnesota and northern Iowa for McClellan Studios.

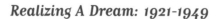

On the Road, On Their Own

Though the opportunities were vast, the work was hard. The photographers traveled icy or dusty and always bumpy country roads, calling on as many as 10 schoolhouses every day. Sales ran between $3 and $6 at each stop, which was enough to make a decent living. But in 1936, opportunity again played into Rothgeb and Reinecker's hands when the owner of McClellan Studios decided to retire and close his business.

Twenty-year-old Eldy Rothgeb and 26-year-old Bruce Reinecker began making plans to start their own school photography company. They chose Minnesota, still predominantly rural with many one-room schools, as their first territory. In August 1937, they sold most of their possessions, pooled their money to buy a car, and headed north. They had $500 in start-up money and a strong belief in the future of their enterprise — National School Studios, School Photography of Distinction. They rented a 1,000-square-foot office for $35 a month above the Baltimore Dairy Lunch at 321 Hennepin Avenue in downtown Minneapolis (now the site of the Minneapolis Public Library). They commissioned William Schwartz of Artistic Furniture to build their first camera — a mahogany box with one lens and a manual film advance. Then they both got married: Rothgeb to Dorothy Sturgis, Reinecker to Vye Nelson. To save money, the couples shared the car and a one-bedroom, $40-a-month apartment. When both men were in Minneapolis, the couples took 12-hour shifts sleeping and working.

National School Studios' first home was a second-floor studio at 321 Hennepin Avenue.

ELDON ROTHGEB

Eldon Rothgeb, the original Lifetouch "picture man," was a salesman's salesman. From his earliest days on the road with Bruce Reinecker until his death in 1972, Rothgeb's heart was with the sales force he had built and nurtured. "Eldy was at his best when he was surrounded by a bunch of the boys in sales," said Richard Erickson in 1986.

During the 1940s, Rothgeb often held impromptu sales meetings over lunch at Charlie's Cafe in downtown Minneapolis. "Before you knew it, 15 or 20 salesmen were eating, talking, and having a good time," Loren Johnson, retired territory manager, recalled in 1986. "Rothgeb was always at the center, enjoying himself while he conducted business. He settled complaints, negotiated deals, and somehow kept everything straight in his mind. He was brilliant. And you couldn't help but like him."

> "He was a father figure to many salesmen."
>
> Richard Erickson

A warm, gregarious man, Rothgeb was also a tough manager with a keen intuition that told him when to prod and when to encourage members of the sales team. As a result, admiration and respect for Rothgeb among the salesmen knew no bounds. "He was not only my boss," said Joe Bianchi in 1986, "he was my benefactor. He had a way of leading and teaching and consoling people that made it a pleasure to work with him."

Rothgeb's management style was impossible to replicate after his death. Instead, National School Studios turned to a management team that focused more on structural strength than on the talents of the individual. Times had changed, requiring new approaches, but as Richard Erickson said in 1986: "Eldy was the right man for the right time. We couldn't have gotten here without him."

Eldon Rothgeb (second from right) was a dedicated golfer.

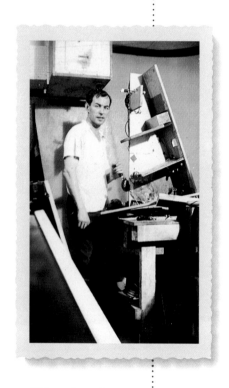

In 1939, NSS employee Ray Blood posed with "Big Bertha," the company's first printer.

Learning the Ropes

Before National School Studios could do business, the partners had to learn more about developing film and printing pictures. Luckily, they met Kodak representative Jimmy Northmore, who taught them the technical knowledge they needed. "I don't know what we'd have done without Jimmy," said Reinecker years later. "He helped us design the developing equipment and then showed us how to use it." Northmore also kept their spirits up during those exhausting early days. "By 10 or 11 at night, everyone would be dead tired, ready to quit," said Reinecker. "But Jimmy always convinced us to finish the work."

In the beginning, Reinecker and Rothgeb handled all the developing and printing themselves. In the darkroom, they wound 200 feet of film onto racks, which were placed in a tank of developer. When the negatives were ready, they printed the pictures one at a time on cut paper, using a wooden printer and a 150-watt bulb, which they controlled with a pulley that moved the bulb back and forth. They put the prints through a stop bath, two hypo baths, three washes, then hung them up to dry. Finally, they matched the prints to the negatives to make sure each school received the proper shipment. The process took nearly three weeks.

Living Up to the Name

With production problems under control, Rothgeb and Reinecker settled into a routine: They called on schools during the day and processed pictures at the office in the evening. They lived up to the "national" in their company's name by hiring Reinecker's younger brother, Bill, to cover the Michigan territory. "They trained me for maybe 30 minutes. Then I put the equipment in the car and drove off," Bill Reinecker said in 1986. Like the training, his equipment was rudimentary — the camera, a tripod, and a reflector to position window light on the subject's face.

For several years, Bill Reinecker and other National School Studios salesmen sold one product — a strip of 13 prints, each 1⅜″ x 2″, priced at 20 cents for three prints, 35 cents for six, or 50 cents for 12. The baker's dozen print was given to the teacher for free — the first of many incentives. Reinecker moved from county to county, calling on 10 to 15 schools a day. Teachers or principals usually accepted his no-risk, no-obligation offer, whereupon Reinecker-the-salesman turned into Reinecker-the-photographer and began shooting.

At the end of each day, Reinecker wrapped and mailed his film to Minneapolis. After processing at NSS, the prints were mailed to the schools, where the students and their parents made their purchases. The teacher mailed the unsold pictures and the money back to Minneapolis. Reinecker's account was credited at 40 percent for each sale and the school received a 10 percent commission (another NSS incentive). The entire transaction took about a month.

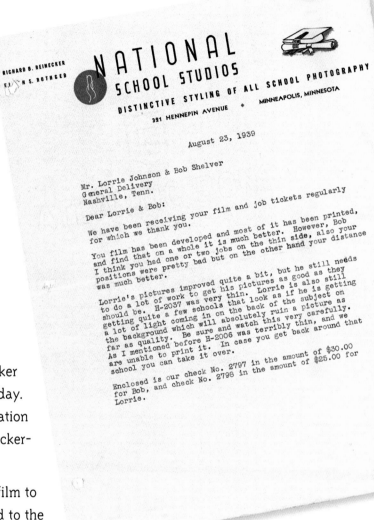

By 1939, more than a dozen salesmen represented NSS in the Upper Midwest. Along with a weekly expense check, salesmen could count on advice from the home office to help them improve sales and photo quality.

BRUCE REINECKER

*B*y the time he was 14 years old, Richard Bruce Reinecker was ready to test his entrepreneurial gift. "I couldn't wait to get out on my own, and I wanted to set the world on fire," Reinecker recalled in 1986. Though he traded a formal education for the business world, his natural curiosity kept him and his company growing for decades. Technology intrigued him. In NSS's early days, Reinecker absorbed the new production techniques provided by Kodak representative Jimmy Northmore. During the war, Reinecker recognized the importance of new technological breakthroughs in film developing and printing, and adapted them to NSS's needs, dramatically increasing production capabilities and efficiencies. "If he didn't have the equipment he needed, Bruce would go out and invent it," said a Kodak representative.

Reinecker's enthusiasm for learning was matched only by his generosity.

"No man is an island" was his philosophy, which he demonstrated in 1978 when he turned the company over to its employees by creating the Lifetouch ESOP. His reasons were simple: "I wanted to reward the people who . . . spent their lives working hard for this company." When the plan went into effect, Reinecker canceled any claims to further compensation. "In 1978, Bruce became a dollar-a-year-man," said Lifetouch veteran Steve Subak.

The ESOP has made Lifetouch stronger than ever. It is an enduring tribute to the company's founder. "I think the ESOP was the most beautiful event ever conceived for the company," said longtime territory manager Clif Erickson. "It united this company."

Reinecker's act of generosity was right in character. His respect for the individual kept him on a first-name basis with employees. His office door was always open. "He was not just an employer, he was a wonderful friend and confidante," said territory manager Joe Bianchi after Reinecker's death in 1987. "And he was like that with 3,500 people."

"This is a great land of opportunity, and I intend to make the most of it. I expect to retire by the time I'm 30."

R. Bruce Reinecker, age 15.

When the U.S. entered World War II, Bruce Reinecker joined the war effort, leaving NSS in the care of his partner, Eldon Rothgeb.

Steve Subak was an accountant with First National Bank in 1938 when he starting moonlighting for NSS as a part-time bookkeeper. In 1994, Subak is still with Lifetouch as customer relations supervisor.

By 1939, more than a dozen salesmen were working for NSS, calling on schools all day and eating on the run. Some tried to shoot 200 pictures a day, no easy task when many schools had only one room and six to 30 students. The salesmen received a $30 draw each week for lodging, food, and gasoline. At the end of each school year, NSS paid their commissions in a lump sum.

Growing the Business

In National School Studios' first year, sales hit $17,200 with a profit of $1,021. In 1938, sales tripled to $65,500 and profits soared to $10,800. The company doubled its space to accommodate 15 employees and, a year later, rented stockroom and warehouse space on the next floor. In 1939, a sales increase of only $4,000 prompted the partners to spur sales by introducing new products: 3″ x 5″ enlargements and display folders.

As the company grew, Rothgeb and Reinecker divided their duties: Reinecker handled production, Rothgeb supervised sales. Neither partner was adept at finance, as First National Bank accountant Steve Subak discovered when, considering their loan application, he perused their books. "They handed me a checkbook and a deposit book. That was it," Subak said. He constructed NSS's first financial statement and approved a $400 loan. He then became their part-time bookkeeper, supplementing his full-time job.

NSS introduced hand-tinted
sepiatone prints in the 1940s.

The War Years

When Bruce Reinecker celebrated his 30th birthday, he received a
cryptic letter from his father: "Dear Son, are you ready to retire? Your
Dad." Reinecker smiled, remembering his youthful boast, yet there was
no denying his success. NSS's sales surpassed $100,000 in 1940, a sub-
stantial achievement considering its highest-priced product sold for
65 cents. The following year, sales hit $159,900, thanks to the efforts
of new staff and a new product — school yearbooks. But when the
United States declared war on Japan and Germany, most of the sales
force joined the armed forces, as did Reinecker, his production assistant Carl Satre, and Steve Subak. By 1943, sales had dropped by
$17,000, the first and only drop in NSS history.

Nationwide, rationing of photographic supplies and gasoline forced
many of NSS's competitors out of business. Yet strokes of luck and genius
helped NSS survive and prosper. The luck derived from a mistake Bruce
Reinecker made. He had given the government figures on the amount
of film and photographic paper the company had used the previous
year. "My arithmetic was never very good and somehow I doubled the
amount of supplies," he said in 1986. These numbers determined the
company's allocation and, as a result, NSS was well supplied.

The stroke of genius came from a persevering Illinois salesman named
Orlyn Carlson, who cracked the city schools in Chicago. Rothgeb immediately turned Carlson's success into a marketing strategy. He pulled
his salesmen from their rural territories, where they were hobbled by

Bruce Reinecker at Pearl
Harbor, Hawaii, 1944.

After World War II, Bruce Reinecker came home to his family and his NSS partner, Eldon Rothgeb.

gas rationing, and sent them to Chicago. Said Bill Reinecker, who joined the effort: "Once I got to Chicago, I was busy every minute. Nearly all the salesmen were taking 800 to 1,200 shots a day."

Handling city schools ultimately changed the company's overall strategy. NSS started booking schools in advance and put more emphasis on services, such as extra pictures for school records. Business thrived, and 1945 sales soared to $330,000.

Boom Years, Bust Profits

With the war over and Reinecker home, the partners made plans to move to a new, larger facility and to rebuild the sales force. The problem was cars. Many of the returning veterans could not afford a car, a job necessity. Reinecker and Rothgeb mortgaged their property and stretched the company's credit line to buy 50 used cars, which they sold to their salesmen on no-interest loans. They made similar loans available for other purchases as well. "After the war," Bill Reinecker recalled, "probably 80 to 85 percent of the salesmen who bought houses got their down payments from the company."

The sales force and NSS's geographic reach grew quickly. Forty salesmen attended the firm's 1946 sales meeting; 120 attended in 1947. NSS expanded beyond the Upper Midwest into 13 states, from Florida and New York in the East to Washington and California in the West.

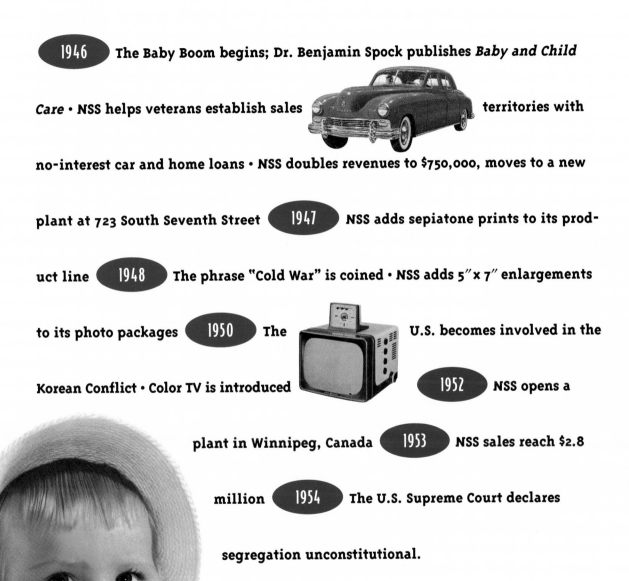

1946 The Baby Boom begins; Dr. Benjamin Spock publishes *Baby and Child Care* • NSS helps veterans establish sales territories with no-interest car and home loans • NSS doubles revenues to $750,000, moves to a new plant at 723 South Seventh Street **1947** NSS adds sepiatone prints to its product line **1948** The phrase "Cold War" is coined • NSS adds 5" x 7" enlargements to its photo packages **1950** The U.S. becomes involved in the Korean Conflict • Color TV is introduced **1952** NSS opens a plant in Winnipeg, Canada **1953** NSS sales reach $2.8 million **1954** The U.S. Supreme Court declares segregation unconstitutional.

By the end of 1947, NSS's tinting department was the company's largest, with 20 workers in the plant and 250 working part-time at home.

By 1947, sales topped $1 million, but the high cost of growth reduced profits to $7,600. Then in 1948, NSS lost $50,000 on sales of $1.4 million. "We grew so fast that all our money went for new equipment and expansion," said Eldon Rothgeb years later. "We were financing the company and the salesmen, so even in a good year, we were in the red."

Cash flow problems forced Rothgeb to borrow $30,000 from a friend to meet the 1946-47 payroll. In 1948, the chairman of the company's bank, First National Bank of Minneapolis, somehow found out that Rothgeb enjoyed high-stakes golf and card games. Recalled Steve Subak: "He advised his board to cancel NSS's credit line in August, right before the school season." Subak, who had become a full-time NSS employee after returning from World War II, helped Rothgeb and Reinecker find a sympathetic ear (and another line of credit) at Northwestern National Bank. "We stayed with them from then on," Subak said.

Revolution in Technology

Postwar growth dramatically expanded NSS's sales force and its production capacity as well. A new 10,000-square-foot plant at 723 South Seventh Street opened for the 1946-47 season. It was five times larger than the old one and "an ingenious marvel of mass production," according to a local business magazine. Stainless steel equipment gleamed everywhere. Pako rockers, which automatically agitated prints through six fixing baths, had replaced hand processing.

Even so, Bruce Reinecker was not satisfied. During the war, he had met William Houston, whose company, Houston-Fearless, had developed a

NSS PRODUCTION PULLS THEM BACK

Women have dominated Lifetouch production positions since the company's founding, but most never planned to stay more than a year. They were seasonal workers who signed on for the fall rush to earn Christmas money or to fill a temporary gap before finding more permanent employment. But the flexible schedule and fun-filled atmosphere brought many women back year after year. Today, the Minneapolis plant abounds with women boasting 20 to 40 years on the job.

"There's something magnetic about the company," said Bernie Niska, who began in 1967. "I guess it has happened to all of us. We've become attached to Lifetouch."

Today, production at Lifetouch NSS relies on an experienced female crew that prints, cuts, packs, and ships pictures at breakneck speed. While female supervisors were pretty rare in the early days, the plant today is staffed with women supervisors who have years of experience. Production manager Dianne Schueller came to Lifetouch as a packer 30 years ago. Today, she manages 150 people on peak season by "making sure the product is moving and people are in the right place at the right time — and sometimes by being either a father confessor or a punching bag."

Bruce Reinecker brought new technologies back to NSS after the war.

continuous film processor for the motion picture industry that automatically and rapidly moved film from solution to solution at appropriate intervals.

Reinecker was eager to acquire this new technology, which he believed would revolutionize the school photography business. He spent two months and nearly $5,000 with Houston-Fearless engineers in Los Angeles before returning to NSS with the equipment.

Next, Reinecker set out to improve the printing end of the process. During the war, the government's V-mail system lowered the cost of sending mail overseas by microfilming letters, mailing the film, and printing it with an Airgraph enlarger. This process was 10 times faster than NSS's method of printing on single cut sheets of paper.

Reinecker asked Kodak, V-mail's inventor, to construct a system big enough to handle NSS's volume. "They told me I was crazy," Reinecker recalled in 1986. "But my friend, Charlie Green, finally convinced Kodak to work on the problem." Kodak and NSS employees adapted the equipment for NSS use, and the change in efficiency was tremendous. "With cut paper, a worker could turn out maybe 800 to 1,000 prints in an eight-hour shift," Reinecker said. "Using a roll of paper and continuous printing and processing, the same worker could turn out 10,000 prints."

With the new production equipment in place, NSS was prepared for a spurt in sales growth, and the company examined its product lines for new opportunities. In 1947, NSS introduced sepiatone enlargements —

SIZE 3½" x 5½" →
HAND-COLORED
SEPIA-TONED ENLARGEMENT
IN FOLDER
50¢

brown-tinted prints, which were popular at small photo studios but had never been offered by a school photography firm. Customers loved them. The sepiatone department became the plant's largest, with 20 plant employees and 250 women working at home.

In 1948, the company introduced 5" x 7" enlargements, which immediately proved another winner. Sales increased to $1.4 million and a year later rose to $2 million. Employing 400 people, including more than 100 salesmen in 48 states, NSS was the largest school photography firm in the country. Despite its astonishing growth, the company retained its informal, friendly, and personal atmosphere.

The Fifties: Brave New Worlds

In the early 1950s, Kodak developed a new process that streamlined color photo development, and small commercial photo finishers dove into the market. However, the high-volume needs of school photography temporarily kept NSS and its competitors out of the market. Most people in the industry believed that consumers were satisfied with black-and-white or sepiatone pictures. National School Studios believed otherwise, and led the way into the color market in 1955.

Being a leader has its risks. Customer acceptance of the higher-priced product was untested, and costs for processing, equipment, and supplies were high. The film had to be hand processed, since continuous processors had not yet been designed. The company's first color prints developed at a rate of five inches per minute, four times slower than

Parents loved sepiatone enlargements in 1947, and they were thrilled when NSS introduced color in 1955.

NSS was able to stay ahead of the competition with higher quality color photographs.

black-and-white. Despite the drawbacks, NSS added color to 36,000 photo packages during the spring of 1956. The following summer, the company installed its first color print processor, which at 18 inches per minute, tripled processing speed.

Next came the hurdle of selling customers on expensive color photos. Black-and-white package prices ranged from $2 to $2.50. The first color package cost $3.50. Selling schools on the new product was also difficult. With black-and-white film, the salesmen could offer a school 14 free services, including identification cards and yearbook pictures. Salesmen could offer only one free service with color because the negatives deteriorated after several printings.

Jim Pool, a salesman in Missouri in the 1950s, wryly summed up the challenges of selling color: "First, you told the customer you were going to give him fewer pictures. Then you told him it would cost more money. Finally, you explained that the school would be getting only one free service. It took a little salesmanship to overcome those obstacles."

Yet customers loved color. National School Studios quickly perfected its quality and production techniques and lowered costs to secure dominance in the market. NSS conducted special training sessions for its sales force on color-shooting techniques to ensure high quality and switched from floodlights to strobe lights to provide better light. In 1957, NSS introduced the Model 10 camera to replace the wooden box cameras that were still standard equipment. With its detachable film magazine, the Model 10 allowed photographers to change film quickly.

The Model 10 also improved lighting control, film metering, and centering. Developed by Stan Merz of Photo Control Company in Minneapolis, the Model 10 evolved into the Photo Control Model 5 camera, which remained the industry standard for 20 years.

At the same time, NSS developed a package printer, which could make multiple prints in different sizes. A student's entire photo package could be printed at once. The new printer improved quality and saved time and money, so NSS could keep prices competitive.

NSS further reduced production costs by switching to on-site paper slitting in 1959. Before this, Kodak, the paper supplier, cut the rolls before shipment. When NSS asked Kodak to ship uncut paper, Kodak didn't have the equipment to comply. NSS turned to DuPont, which sold NSS master rolls and a used slitter. The savings came to nearly $50,000 a year.

By the end of the 1950s, NSS was by far the dominant company in the school photography market. The addition of color paid off handsomely. Between 1957 and 1959, NSS's sales shot from $3 million to $4.2 million. Why? Everyone loved color.

NSS's rapid growth and innovation attracted industry-wide attention in the mid-1950s.

In 1950, sales representatives for National School Studios display the company's products at an East Coast sales convention.

In 1965, NSS converted a bowling alley in Derby, Connecticut, into its East Coast production facility.

The Houses That NSS Built

While great strides were being made in production and sales, National School Studios also expanded facilities to accommodate growth. In 1952, NSS opened its first plant outside Minneapolis in Winnipeg, Manitoba, managed and half-owned by Ted Vardalos. (Later, Vardalos became sole owner and eventually sold out to Jostens, Inc.)

Expansion into other markets did not come as easily: In 1955, construction on a plant in Oakland, California, was abandoned due to labor trouble. NSS opened a plant in Reno, Nevada, instead. But when east-coast business grew, NSS decided to close its plant in Reno and open a plant in Derby, Connecticut. Here, NSS capitalized on its previous experiences, working carefully to bring the new plant up to full capacity. Even so, "the first run in 1965 was a fiasco," recalled Fred Gowan, then New York and Vermont territory manager. "Most of the schools I shot in September weren't delivered until late February." Two years later, Derby was processing 1.2 million photo packages, more than double Reno's volume after a decade.

By the early 1960s, National School Studios was breaking records: Sales topped $5 million in 1961, $6 million in 1964. Markets included all 50 states, Puerto Rico, Canada, Germany, and Sweden.

1955 NSS's West Coast operations begin • U.S. agrees to train South

Vietnamese army Richard Erickson joins NSS in Michigan •

Bill Haley records "Rock Around the Clock" and launches Rock

and Roll **1956** NSS introduces color school photos • Elvis Presley takes the

country by storm with his first hit, "Heartbreak Hotel" **1957**

NSS introduces package printing and the Model 10 camera • Russia

launches Sputnik and the U.S. enters the race for the moon **1959** NSS saves

$50,000 per year by slitting paper on-site **1960** NSS

initiates new chargeback system **1963** President

Kennedy is assassinated in Dallas, Texas.

THE SALES FORCE

*S*ince 1937, friends, family, and fate have led many young entrepreneurs to the Lifetouch sales force. "You've got your freedom, you're your own boss," said Fred Gowan, who enjoyed having his summers to fish at his Michigan cabin. Selling for Lifetouch was also a lot of fun. "You had to enjoy it, or you wouldn't stay in the business," said Lifetouch board chairman and CEO Richard Erickson.

Selling wasn't all fun and games. The sales season lasted only four to five months for many years, and there wasn't a moment to spare from Labor Day to Christmas. Salespeople scrambled to sell schools, shoot good photos, and get the packages out the door on schedule. "If you made a mistake, you'd be the one to suffer the consequences," said Gowan.

Some of those consequences, while embarrassing at the time, live on as funny stories of lessons learned in the field. Richard Erickson learned his lesson his first day on the job in Kalamazoo, Michigan. When he delivered his day's work to his brother Clif, who had hired him to help with a large territory, he found there was no film in the camera — and hadn't been all day. "I had to go back the next day and take all the pictures over again," said Erickson. "This time I made sure there was film in the camera."

NSS salesmen gathered in 1938 for the company's first annual sales meeting.

In 1967, bursting at the seams in its old facility, National School Studios bought an eight-acre site in Bloomington, a growing suburb south of Minneapolis. In September 1968, Mortenson Construction completed a new 72,000-square-foot plant. For safety's sake, NSS ran both plants during the 1968 fall season. The problems of tracking orders, matching quality, and hauling supplies were unnerving. Seasoned employees worked grueling 16-hour shifts to get the work done, a memory that prompted many to recall 1968 as the toughest year in the company's history.

In September 1968, NSS moved into a new 72,000-square-foot plant in Bloomington, Minnesota.

Coming of Age: 1960-1972

The new plant helped NSS meet its next challenge — inflation. The plant's efficiency helped offset increased supply and labor costs. Yet package prices continued to rise, forcing NSS to examine its speculation payment system. Since the beginning, NSS had processed complete packages of photos for every student. The student and his or her parents then decided whether or not to buy — and the unsold packages were discarded. Because nearly 20 percent of the packages did not sell, the cost of discarded paper and wasted processing time became increasingly burdensome. In 1965, NSS moved, somewhat reluctantly, to a pre-pay system.

Besides photographs, National School Studios supplied schools with photographic accessories.

Pre-Pay Saves the Day

Many salespeople didn't want to abandon speculation. But Michigan territory manager Clif Erickson devised a reasoned approach: "People were becoming concerned about the environment. I touted pre-pay because it conserved resources." And it did: NSS saved paper, chemicals, and the fuel needed to run the equipment and to ship unsold packages back and forth. Schools benefited also because teachers no longer had to collect money or oversee package returns. By 1966, pre-pay was the preferred method of operation.

In 1968, NSS introduced another new product — the 8″ x 10″ enlargement. Demand for 8″ x 10″s doubled in 1969, then quadrupled in 1970. "The 8″ x 10″ was absolutely vital to our success in the late 1960s and early 1970s," said Lifetouch CEO Richard Erickson. "It doubled our package price, nearly doubled sales, and, I believe, doubled customer satisfaction."

The New National School Studios Building at Highways 494-100

Largest Photo School Firm Booms

National School Studios, Inc. is one of many companies that have moved to the suburbs, because they need more elbow-room.

National is the world's largest photography company producing student portraits exclusively for schools. The firm began its move to the new 72,000-square-foot plant off I-494 last fall. "We moved in officially on December 23," said E. S. Rothgeb, president.

Rothgeb, an Edina resident, is the photographer's photographer. His short-cropped hair and burly frame magnify his athletic agressiveness. A fire-engine red sport coat signals persistence and energy that won't quit.

Bloomington extended a friendly hand to its new tax-paying denizen. National's address was changed to Picture Drive from the previous Yosemite Avenue.

THE NEW PLANT places the firm on solid footing for future growth. National's marketing area includes all 50 states along with Puerto Rico and parts of Europe. Present facilities are about three times larger than the previous plant at 723 S. 7th Street, Minneapolis which was 25,000 square feet. About 300 work at the new plant in the busy fall season. Another plant in Derby, Conn., doing finishing work only, employs 100. Affiliated with the Bloomington headquarters are 160 salesmen-photographers who call on schools throughout the country.

Sales at the number one school shutterbug were about $9 million in 1968, said Rothgeb. He estimates about $10 million, this year. Last year, the firm snapped about eight million smiling faces. From these photos, about 160 million prints were made of

youngsters, grinning at the bright lights with the word "cheese" glued between their teeth.

ABOUT 70 PERCENT of prints are sold, according to Rothgeb. The firm returns finished prints, not sample proofs, to students and their families. Of the total number sold, 30 percent are black-and-white, and 70 percent are in color.

National sales people get their foot in the door by offering services to schools. Pictures are provided for school records, student identification cards, year books and teacher incentive plans in the classroom.

Because schools have immediate use for pictures, and since parents use them at Christmas, the busy shutter season is in the fall. The portrait spectrum extends through 12th grade, said Rothgeb. In the elementary years, parents provide a big

demand. In high school, teen-age egos take over.

Along with Rothgeb, major officers in the shutterbug outfit are R. Bruce Reinecker of Minnetonka, vice president; Steven Subak of Edina, secretary-treasurer; Carl W. Satre of Osseo, plant manager; and technical advisors of sales, Robert P. Savage of Minnetonka and Stan Hanson of Bloomington. The last two divide their operative domains at the Mississippi River.

THE COMPANY had its beginning in 1936 in an upstairs plant over the old Baltimore Dairy Lunch on Hennepin Ave., Minneapolis. Equipment consisted of two contact printers made of wood.

In 1946, the firm moved to its location that preceded the recent move to a site on Interstate 494 west of Highway 100. The first continuous processor in the photo-

graphic industry was installed there in 1949.

Processing machines, installed side-by-side, fill the entire width of the new plant. The entire developing process, including cutting is almost completely automated. Chemicals are gravity-fed from vats on the second level.

Color processing machines cost up to $25,000 each, according to Satre, plant manager. Multi-printed shots, produced in size and number specified by individual schools, come off driers with mirror-like fidelity.

The way things are "shaping up" at the new plant, National people could look at the "birdie" with a pretty big smile.

Rothgeb Reinecker

By 1969, an efficient new plant and innovative new products kept NSS growing at a spectacular rate.

Clif Erickson
in 1950.

CLIF ERICKSON
Life of the Picture Man

Like many Lifetouch sales veterans, Clif Erickson joined the company after finishing college on the GI bill. "I applied for work in 1949 the day after Labor Day, the worst time in the world in this industry, because everybody was hired by then," he said. But a position opened up in Michigan when an NSS salesman was injured in an accident. Erickson was granted the territory for the season and stayed for 41 years.

Like other salespeople, Erickson spent his days combing country roads, visiting 10 to 15 one-room schoolhouses, selling to the teachers and shooting photos on the spot. Helping kids look their best was part of the job. "We'd pull down the bibs on the overalls, smooth shirts, and fix collars. Some salespeople carried bow ties," he said. Erickson was also a master at winning smiles. "You had to have the ability to get kids into the palm of your hand," he said. His own children kept him well-stocked with funny sayings guaranteed to get a grin at the crucial moment.

By the time Erickson retired in 1990, many changes had transformed the life of the "picture man." Paved roads and school consolidations, pre-pay and a variety of products, the Micro-Z camera and digital imaging all added up to a very different world of school photography. But for Clif Erickson, the essence of the job remained the same. "I loved to make people laugh and to help kids have a great day," he said.

1965 NSS sales top $5 million **1966** The federal government

establishes Medicare for the elderly • Pre-pay replaces speculation as NSS's

payment method **1968**  Martin Luther King, Jr., and Robert

F. Kennedy are assassinated • NSS builds a new office and plant in

Bloomington, Minnesota **1969** Apollo astronaut Neil

Armstrong becomes the first man to walk on the moon

1970 The National Guard kills four student antiwar demonstrators at

Kent State University **1972** Eldon Rothgeb dies suddenly • Bruce

Reinecker appoints Richard Erickson vice president of sales and

marketing • President Nixon visits Moscow for summit talks.

The Crisis

National School Studios came through the turbulent 1960s with impressive financial figures: Although supply and labor costs had more than doubled, and inflation showed no signs of abating, sales grew to $10 million and profits remained steady. But on March 30, 1972, all of NSS's past and present problems suddenly paled when president and co-founder Eldon Rothgeb died unexpectedly of a heart attack at age 55. Rothgeb's death seemed a mortal blow to the company, too. Many employees saw Rothgeb as the dominant partner, particularly among the sales force, because of his hands-on management style and Reinecker's frequent absences to manage the Reno operation. "He was a father figure to many salesmen," Richard Erickson recalled.

Bruce Reinecker had little time to mourn the loss of his friend and partner of 38 years. "No one man can fill Eldy Rothgeb's shoes," he wrote in a memo to concerned and anxious employees. "But I am going to head a team that is sure as hell going to try." One thing he was not going to do was sell National School Studios to another company: "I think I should make my thoughts clear to you…" he wrote to numerous hopefuls in January 1975. "There are more than 1,000 people in my company, many of whom have never worked for anyone else….Loyalty is something that cannot be bought or bartered. It must be earned, and in this area my people and I have a beautiful relationship. Therefore, please be advised that my company is not for sale now or in the future."

At National School Studios, an era had come to an end in a heartbeat.

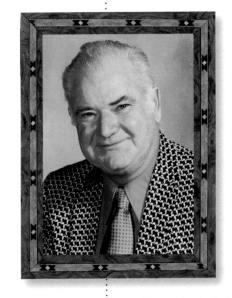

Eldon Rothgeb died suddenly of a heart attack at age 55.

KEEP
AMERICA
BEAUTIFUL
SUPPORT
MINI-SKIRTS

72

KIDS
are
#1
with
National
School
Studios

MEMORIES

"Dedicated to Preserving Memories"

THE DREAM

Between 1972 and 1979, National School Studios continued to prosper under the leadership of its surviving founder, Bruce Reinecker. As the nation's leading school photography company, NSS saw its sales grow from $14 million to $32 million, and its profits triple. The company acquired Prestige Portraits and Universal Publications, expanded operations, and added new products. NSS overcame inflation and increased efficiency with a company-wide waste control program. And with the stroke of a pen in 1978, Bruce Reinecker realized his dream of turning National School Studios over to his employees.

1972 to 1979

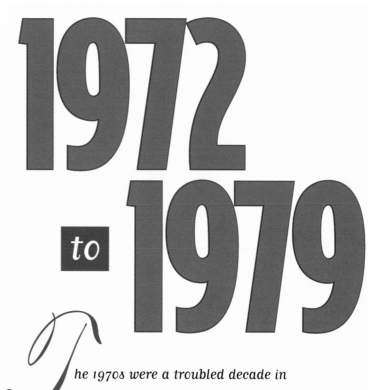

The 1970s were a troubled decade in America, marked by the war in Vietnam and a government scandal that led to the resignation of the president. In 1975, the United States retreated from Vietnam and disillusioned soldiers returned to a nation suffering from an energy crisis, double-digit inflation, and an economic recession that left many people out of work. The nation's optimism returned with the bicentennial, symbolized by the restored Statue of Liberty. But most Americans had to wait until the 1980s to see those symbols of hope become a reality.

1972 The price of a home in the Midwest averages $29,300 • Bruce Reinecker creates the NSS Sales Advisory Board **1973** OPEC imposes an oil embargo on the U.S., Western Europe, and Japan • The Beatles begin solo careers with Paul McCartney touring his band "Wings" **1974** NSS institutes its first employee recognition program and acquires Prestige Portraits of Muncie, Indiana • The Watergate scandal forces President Richard Nixon to resign from office **1975** NSS acquires Universal Publications of Kansas City, Missouri • Emergency helicopters evacuate the last 1,000 Americans from South Vietnam, ending 20 years of military involvement.

Senior class president Richard Erickson planned to go into farming after he graduated from Winthrop High School in the early 1950s. In 1955, he joined NSS as a photographer. By 1976, he was executive vice president.

Setting a New Course

When Eldon Rothgeb died, the National School Studios sales force was working in every state and several foreign countries. Rothgeb had been the linchpin that held the sales organization together, and choosing a new leader for the sales force was a difficult and demanding task. No one could fill Eldy's shoes, yet someone had to take over and provide strong leadership. Bruce Reinecker, demonstrating his own sharp instincts, appointed Ohio territory manager Richard Erickson to the newly created position of vice president for sales and marketing. Though Erickson had joined the company in 1955, following his brother Clif, he was still considered a newcomer by many NSS salesmen. Reinecker was convinced, however, that leadership potential was not measured by longevity. He saw in Erickson a combination of strength and experience that could move the company forward. "I knew we had to make changes," Reinecker said in 1986, "because my style and Eldy's differed and because the company had grown and needed to change. I wanted someone who wasn't tied to the old ways, yet who had enough experience with the company to appreciate what we had accomplished."

Reinecker and Erickson built a solid working relationship and forged a new vision for NSS, mindful of the past while focused on the future. "We wanted to keep the things that had made the company great — the closeness, the support, the individual initiative," Erickson said. "And we wanted to introduce some defined management principles to help us plan for more consistent growth and profit levels."

44

A Delegating Style

Erickson and Reinecker created a new management style that gave employees broader responsibilities for day-to-day decision making. Delegating authority was a distinct departure from Rothgeb's traditional entrepreneurial approach, which necessitated his involvement in every aspect and detail of the business. "Rothgeb ran the business out of his hip pocket," said retired territory manager Loren Johnson in 1986. "He was sharp enough to do it, but the company was getting too big to run that way much longer."

Also in 1972, Reinecker established an Advisory Board to expand the leadership of the sales organization. The board was responsible for keeping management informed on existing or potential problems, possible solutions, and areas needing improvement.

The Sales NSS Advisory Board gave the people in the field a more active voice in their company and signalled Reinecker's inclusive management approach. He believed in the importance of delegating authority and practiced it often. At the same time he appointed Erickson vice president for sales and marketing, Reinecker gave greater responsibility for finance to Steve Subak and for plant operations to Carl Satre.

Members of the NSS Advisory Board met in January 1973. They are (clockwise from far right) Bruce Reinecker, Hal Ridges, Fred Gowan, George Finkboner, Dick Lidholm, Pete Williams, Harold Orth, and Joe May.

By the 1970s, product packages included "9-up" photos like those shown above. In 1974, NSS initiated an employee recognition plan honoring length of service. Recipients were awarded specially designed NSS jewelry.

"Reinecker believed in getting competent people and then letting them do their work and report the results to him," said Subak.

For Richard Erickson, the authority he suddenly shouldered was a monumental challenge: "I came in as a very experienced territory man but a totally inexperienced executive," he recalled. "There was a lot of work to do, and I had to learn every problem first-hand. I couldn't delegate my authority right off. If I had, I never would have learned my job."

Rewarding Good Work

In 1974, Reinecker instituted a company-wide recognition program to encourage and acknowledge employee contributions. Outlining his reasons in a January memo, he wrote, "Many of you have told me that we are more than a company — we are a family. With that in mind, I wanted to create a symbol that could be worn proudly by all of us, something that was not available to anyone else in the world, something that could not be bought but had to be earned." The original awards — 14-karat gold rings and bracelets, studded with emeralds or diamonds — were given to employees in recognition of their length of service, and they were worn with pride.

Reinecker also wanted to reward his employees financially. But in the early and mid-1970s, the company lacked the funds. "We were a $9 million company at the time," Reinecker said, "and there's no way you can reward 500 to 600 people from the profits of a $9 million company — it's just not in the books." To accomplish his goal, Reinecker and Erickson discussed strategies to increase NSS's profitability.

"We wanted to be able to go into a school and take care of all its photographic needs — yearly school photos, senior portraits, and annuals," Erickson recalled. They decided to focus on acquiring companies with compatible products, and chose Prestige Portraits as the first major acquisition.

Birds of a Feather

The two companies were already well acquainted. Prestige Portraits had opened its doors in the late 1940s, at a time when National School Studios was cutting costs with new wartime production technologies and gaining new customers with sepiatone enlarge-

ments. Specializing in portraits of high school seniors, Prestige was founded in Muncie, Indiana, by Jim and John Reid, who were later joined by their brother Harold. Although the two companies were in the same business, they were not direct competitors — each filled a separate niche in the school photography market. On occasion, however, their niches overlapped, when a school insisted that NSS supply senior portraits as part of its total package. NSS's inability to do so was detrimental

In 1974, National School Studios acquired Prestige Portraits, of Muncie, Indiana, a $1 million company specializing in senior portraits. In 1979, Prestige Portraits moved into a new facility (above) in Muncie.

Prestige founder John Reid became a valued NSS executive. In 1976, Reid conducted a presentation with Senior Portraits manager John Yount.

to its salespeople, who risked losing the contract if NSS failed to meet the customer's need. In 1954, National School Studios and Prestige Portraits decided to collaborate. When NSS encountered schools that wanted senior portraits, NSS funneled that business to Prestige, which handled the production in its Muncie plant. Prestige, likewise, processed its limited elementary school work through National School Studios' plants. It was a win-win arrangement. Both Prestige and NSS kept accounts they might otherwise have lost and gained new business they might not have had.

By 1974, National School Studios' 20-year association with Prestige made it a natural for acquisition, and the results proved it: A year after National School Studios purchased the $1 million company, Prestige's business doubled. "Joining National School Studios gave us resources that we didn't have," said John Reid. "We were able to expand our production facilities and increase our sales efforts."

In addition to the new company, National School Studios also gained a valuable new executive. Instead of retiring like his brothers, John Reid worked with NSS for more than 10 years, first as president of Prestige and later in a variety of key positions at the Bloomington headquarters.

Products, Processes, and Growth

Nineteen seventy-four was a busy year for NSS. Along with the acquisition of Prestige Portraits, NSS introduced Select-a-Pack, a new sales strategy that gave each school three photo options instead of the single-option "happy medium" package that was too expensive for some customers and provided too few photos for others. With the choice and variety of Select-a-Pack, National School Studios won new customers and increased sales once again.

While Select-a-Pack increased sales, it complicated the photographic process for the NSS sales force. Photographers could no longer quickly round up and photograph a classroom of 30 children. Now they had to photograph each group according to package type: the "A" group first, then the "B" group, followed by the "Cs." Children who did not buy a package were in the "X" group. (They posed only for the school's I.D. shots.) Over time, Select-a-Pack became tough to sell because every student knew what everyone else bought according to the order in which they were photographed. To solve the problem, NSS researched and developed a system for marking the package type on the film, next to the child's name. Photos then could be taken in any order, and the students' choices remained confidential.

Of Codes and Efficiencies

During the turbulent 1970s, National School Studios' ongoing research and development efforts created many new products and processes. In

Select-a-Pack offered NSS customers a variety of photo package options beginning in 1974.

The revolutionary Micro-Z camera thrust NSS into the computer age.

mid-decade, the company developed and patented a process that incorporated the new bar code technology into the photo process. Photographers could now mark the film at the point of sale. "Once we produced reliable bar codes, we started automating," said Gary Goenner, Lifetouch vice president for production. "We hand-wired the color package printers first, then moved on to the new 10" x 13" package printers," he said. At the same time, plant engineers were working to control and improve the color process.

By the late 1970s, National School Studios' Bloomington plant had stepped fully into the computer age: switching from hand-wired, vacuum tube components to printed circuit boards, computer chips, and micro processors. "It was clearly the way for us to go," Goenner said. "The new technology paid off in cost savings and efficiency. It also made us more competitive. We were already the low-cost producer, but we couldn't sit still. So we kept getting more efficient by investing in new systems. We wanted to work smarter, not harder." Eventually, the investments NSS made in computer technology would provide the foundation for a new generation of camera, the Micro-Z.

1976 NSS's new paper conservation program cuts

waste 61 percent in the first year • Mark Kilchenman joins NSS

as a part-time photographer in Michigan **1977** Second baseman Rod Carew

bats team record .388 for Minnesota Twins • Paul Harmel joins NSS as controller

• President Jimmy Carter calls the nation's energy crisis "the moral equivalent of

war" **1978** Bruce Reinecker turns NSS ownership over to employees through

the ESOP **1979** Americans are held hostage at the American

Embassy in Teheran, Iran • Margaret Thatcher

is elected Great Britain's first woman

prime minister.

Universal Publications
in Kansas City, Missouri.

Growing Pains

A year before the acquisition of Prestige Portraits, National School Studios had purchased a controlling interest in Universal Publications, a company in Kansas City, Missouri, that specialized in school yearbooks. By investing in Universal, NSS was attempting to consolidate its school annual business, which up to that time was supplied by several companies. Now NSS channeled all its school annual work through Universal and began to fund Universal's expansion to increase its capacity.

By the start of the 1975-76 school year, Universal had grown into the second floor of its two-story building in Kansas City. But its capabilities were strained when an unprecedented number of orders poured in from the NSS sales force. Although Universal had nearly doubled its space and equipment, few changes had been made in operating procedures. "Systems that worked with 300 contracts blew apart with 2,000," said Richard Erickson. By spring, only six weeks before scheduled delivery, Universal started falling behind on its orders. The company's manager told Erickson they probably wouldn't complete the orders by the end of the school year. Because the annuals were part of a total package sold to schools by NSS, failure to deliver on time would reflect badly on National School Studios, and disgruntled clients might take their business elsewhere. The sales force was getting anxious.

Erickson and Bruce Reinecker dispatched a team of troubleshooters to assess the problem, including Bloomington plant manager Carl Satre and Bob Thompson, then president of Foss Printing. Erickson's assistant, Jim Haeg, went to Kansas City to field phone calls from worried NSS salespeople.

The NSS team identified the production problems and then determined the kind of help needed to produce and ship the annuals on time. The demands were sobering: 56 people were needed to work 12 hours a day, seven days a week, for the next four to six weeks. Carl Satre broke the news to Richard Erickson. After a moment of silence, Erickson said: "Well, let's do whatever it takes."

Satre then called color production manager Bill DeCoursey in Bloomington and asked him to drum up volunteers. Though it was Sunday morning, DeCoursey asked Barb Knolls, head of personnel, to start calling. By 5 p.m., 25 people had volunteered to drop everything and fly to Kansas City. They were soon joined by 25 others. Bruce Reinecker chauffeured workers from the Bloomington plant to the airport. Richard Erickson shuttled workers back and forth in Kansas City. The 50 NSS workers set to work to get the job done, and by season's end, Universal had shipped more than 90 percent of its orders on time.

When all this work was done, National School Studios purchased the remaining Universal stock to ensure complete control of the company. Under George Kmetz, then Bob Thompson, Universal embarked on a program of controlled growth. In 1993, Universal, now named Lifetouch Publishing, opened a second plant in Love's Park, Illinois.

NSS's once-spacious Bloomington plant was at capacity by the early 1970's. In 1974, shipping department manager Stan ("Specs") VanBlaricom kept products moving on the shipping room floor.

JOHN REID

*I*n 1974, when National School Studios acquired Prestige Portraits of Muncie, Indiana, it landed a good company and a top-notch executive — John Reid.

Reid came to headquaters in 1978 to serve as vice president for sales and marketing. He soon developed a close working relationship with Richard Erickson. "John was a rare individual with whom I could bounce ideas back and forth," Erickson recalled. "He could separate himself from his job and ponder with me the future of this company."

In Bloomington, Reid worked on the NSS sales training program and the development of second-sale products. In 1983, he became vice president of corporate development for NSS. In this new capacity, Reid targeted acquisitions, hitting a bull's-eye with Kinderfoto. Later that year, he became interim president of Lifetouch Portrait Studios. Reid retired in 1984.

A Wake-Up Call

Although NSS managed to avert a crisis with the last-minute delivery of the school annuals, the company soon ran into a more severe problem — escalating costs. New products and rising sales had kept inflation at bay for several years. But world events delivered a one-two punch that hammered the company's profits: In 1975, a worldwide silver shortage caused dramatic increases in silver prices, a key ingredient in photographic paper. "One day, Kodak doubled the price of film and doubled the price of chemistry," said Jim Haeg. "Our costs skyrocketed overnight." Even so, NSS was reluctant to increase charges to its sales force because the OPEC oil embargo of 1973, which had triggered spiraling gas prices, was already hurting the company's traveling salespeople.

As a result of these inflationary trends, NSS posted a loss in 1976, the first time in 11 years. Reinecker and Erickson examined the numbers and made a difficult decision: NSS had to raise its charges to the sales force. At the 1976 winter sales meeting, Erickson broke the bad news: The company was increasing chargebacks 25 percent from 72 to 90 points per 3"x5" unit. The sales force was shocked. Chargebacks had increased only once in the past 15 years, and then by only nine points. This increase was double that. "It was a very traumatic time," said territory manager Jim Pool in 1986. "Many salespeople hadn't increased their prices for years. We didn't know whether the schools would accept the increases or whether we'd go broke."

A worldwide silver shortage in 1975 created dramatic cost increases at NSS, but production continued unabated.

But like millions of other American individuals and companies in the inflation-wracked 1970s, National School Studios, its sales force, and its customers absorbed the price increases and moved on. After 1976, NSS adjusted its chargebacks annually to reflect inflation and production costs. With yearly adjustments, drastic new increases were eliminated and territory managers and salespeople became much more attuned to the actual cost of doing business. "Nineteen seventy-six was a tough year," said Jim Pool, "but I think we became better business people as a result."

Waste Not...

All of Lifetouch pitched in to cut paper waste in the 1970s.

Dealing with inflation properly demanded more than an increase in prices. It also demanded a decrease in costs. NSS embarked on a campaign to reduce paper waste, a plan first suggested in 1974. A new type of film printed badly and led to a high makeover rate — up to 25 percent in 1976. As a result, paper waste skyrocketed.

To tackle the company-wide waste problems, NSS brought in Tal Hopson, a consulting engineer who later joined the company as chief of design engineering. Hopson's waste-control program was based on the premise that any material the company bought that wasn't passed on to the customer at a profit constituted waste. Hopson soon involved NSS employees because, he said, "the workers know where the waste is occurring and how to make it go away."

Richard ("Red") Palmquist, then machine maintenance manager, was put in charge of the paper waste program at NSS's Bloomington plant. What he discovered was astonishing: "In 1976, 39 percent of the paper we bought was wasted. That represented seven semi-truck loads of paper at a cost of $1.3 million."

NSS employees attended workshops designed to help them identify waste and understand its costs. Following the workshops, Palmquist formed a 12-member paper waste committee to identify problem areas and suggest solutions. To encourage participation, the company also gave out prizes (paid out of paper waste savings) to NSS plant employees at the annual picnic.

Obviously, the waste program generated its own costs, specifically the tracking system and time off for committee members who attended bimonthly meetings. But the savings realized from the program more than covered these costs. "We calculated that each percentage point of waste represented $40,000," said Dennis Hendren, who eventually took over the paper waste program at the Bloomington plant. "During the first year, our percentage of waste dropped from 39 to 15 percent, a savings of nearly $1 million."

"Before we started the program, production accounted for 50 percent of our sales dollar," said Richard Erickson. "Now it's down to 24.5 percent. By wasting less paper, we've cut our labor costs."

National School Studios' efforts to cut costs paid off in increased profits. With sales rising from $22 million in 1976 to nearly $26 million in 1977, NSS was profitable once again.

39% 15%

Paper Waste Decline in First Year

In the first year of NSS's waste-control program, paper waste dropped 61 percent.

NSS PRODUCTION "FOUNDERS"

From fundamental hand processing to digital technology, Lifetouch's production department has undergone a phenomenal evolution in its 58 years. Through it all, the company's production processes have been guided by five tenacious men, each with 40-plus years of Lifetouch experience. Taken together, these production founders — Red Palmquist, Carl Satre, Jerry Westermann, Dean Wilson, and Bill DeCoursey — represent more than 220 years of experience at Lifetouch.

Red Palmquist joined NSS as a machine maintenance worker in the late 1940s. In more than 40 years, he managed the company's plants in Reno (Nevada), Derby (Connecticut), Chico (California), and Minneapolis before becoming corporate vice president of production. Palmquist retired in 1991.

Carl Satre joined NSS in 1938, at age 15. He worked nights in the company's first studio in downtown Minneapolis, sweeping floors, sorting film, and doing odd jobs. He joined NSS full-time after high school and spent his entire career at Lifetouch, as plant manager in Minneapolis and Derby, and later as director of purchasing. Satre retired in 1983 after 45 years with the company. He died in 1988.

Dean Wilson (above), Carl Satre (left), Bill DeCoursey (right).

In his senior year of high school in 1948, Jerry Westermann took a part-time job in the NSS shipping department. He became a production supervisor in 1959, and held various production positions for the rest of his career. In 1986, Westermann was named vice president of production for NSS's Bloomington and Derby plants. He retired in 1992.

General manager of production Dean Wilson joined NSS in 1949. Like the others, he worked his way up, beginning at the shipping table. He was named Bloomington plant manager and general manager of production in 1976. Wilson continues to provide leadership and direction for the Bloomington production facility.

Bill DeCoursey joined NSS part-time in 1947 while still in high school. He started and managed the color department for NSS in 1955, and spearheaded the company's use of computers by creating NSS's early computer programs. Still going strong after 47 years with Lifetouch, he is now director of safety and environmental concerns.

"Throughout our history, both management and technology have helped our production departments lower costs, improve efficiency, and increase productivity," said Dean Wilson. "Each of us has been dedicated to helping the company grow and be successful, and we've all done our part to make it happen."

Jerry Westermann (standing, left),
Red Palmquist (right).

NSS color class composites preserve childhood memories of friends and teachers.

Cutting Back

NSS's 1976 financial crisis also prompted Reinecker and Erickson to examine the company's management practices. Since 1972, NSS's sales had increased 57 percent. NSS had also tripled its operations, growing from a specialized school photography company to three companies (NSS, Universal Publications, and Prestige Portraits). NSS was offering school photos, senior portraits, and high school annuals. Yet few managerial changes had been made to reflect NSS's substantial growth and expansion.

For example, until 1975, all territory managers reported to Erickson just as they had to Rothgeb since the company's founding. Jim Haeg's appointment as Erickson's assistant helped ease Erickson's workload, but not for long. Within a year, Erickson's duties increased again, and there wasn't enough time in the day to handle them all. "I was sales manager, vice president of sales, and marketing manager," Erickson recalled. "For a five-year period, I was also regional manager, district manager, and national sales manager with 85 territories. Plus I was trying to help on the production side and also integrate Prestige and Universal into NSS. It was a wild time."

In addition, Bruce Reinecker, now 66, knew he had to prepare the company and himself for his retirement. In June 1976, he appointed Erickson executive vice president. To help him tackle the job, Erickson turned to the University of Minnesota, where he participated in the

Minnesota Executive Program, an intensive six-week course in organizational strategy that built on Erickson's finance and management knowledge. "It was the worst possible time to be in the program," Erickson said. "I had no time to spare. Yet it was also the best possible time because so much of what I learned applied to our situation. We'd get case studies and after looking one over, I'd say, 'That's us!' Then I'd read another and say, 'That's us, too!'"

Erickson finished the program determined to move NSS to a new level — from an entrepreneurial to a team-managed organization. "We had wanted to make this change for a long time, but Bruce and I had been reluctant to move too quickly," said Erickson. "We went slowly to cause as little pain as possible. But a slow approach can create problems too. It's like bobbing a dog's tail a little bit at a time so it doesn't hurt as much."

One of Erickson's first additions to the new management team was ElRoy Nerness, a CPA and partner in Boulay, Heutmaker, Zibell & Company, the firm that handled NSS's audits. Nerness had the financial skills NSS needed and a detailed knowledge of the company.

Nerness joined National School Studios in June 1977 and immediately used the company's computer system, installed in 1974, to generate departmental budgets, monthly financial statements, and long-range financial plans. "NSS had never had that type of information before,"

Colorful product literature and an NSS patch worn by company salespeople made National School Studios easily identifiable to school officials in the 1970s.

The new dual image photograph gave NSS salespeople a second-sale opportunity in 1978.

Nerness said. "That wasn't unusual for a company its size, but to move ahead we had to do some forecasting and we had to have a plan."

In 1978, NSS added another manager to the team, appointing John Reid, then president of Prestige Portraits, as vice president of sales and marketing. Reid oversaw the company's 528 salespeople. In 1979, realizing the sales force needed more direct support, Erickson and Reid divided the country into five geographic zones and appointed a manager for each zone to provide backing to the territory managers. In 1980, NSS established an account executive department to provide territory managers with troubleshooters who could handle office or production questions. With Erickson's help, Reid also began to develop a new sales training program.

During this busy period, National School Studios introduced its first "second-sale" product, a creative new photo featuring a dual image on a black background. Offered in the spring of 1978, the new line meant salespeople could book schools twice — once in the fall for regular school photos and again in the spring for the dual image shots. The second sale also gave salespeople who had been unsuccessful in the fall another chance to win clients. The dual image business helped NSS compensate for a dip in sales due to declining school enrollments during the mid- and late 1970s. Though the new business merely bolstered sagging sales at first, the new product boomed in the early 1980s.

Time of Transition

While the new management team was coping with managerial modernization and company growth, Bruce Reinecker was operating behind the scenes to turn the company over to his employees.

In 1973, Reinecker had taken the first step to make his longstanding dream come true by establishing a company profit-sharing plan. New government regulations in 1976, however, forced NSS to discontinue the plan. "I called a meeting with Dick Erickson and ElRoy Nerness," Reinecker recalled, "and told them I was not going to abandon my plan, and that I wanted them to help me find a way to make it happen."

For the next two years, Erickson and Nerness explored various options to come up with a feasible strategy. Then Nerness received information about employee stock ownership trusts (ESOTs) from Menke & Associates, a consulting firm in San Francisco. He called the company and learned that ESOTs were now exempt from the 1976 regulations that had hampered Reinecker's earlier efforts. Nerness and Erickson flew to San Francisco in February 1978 to discuss the plan with Menke specialists. They reported the results of the meeting to Reinecker and he gave Menke & Associates the go-ahead.

Bruce Reinecker announced the company's new ESOP to NSS employees in June 1978.

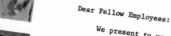

National School Studios, Inc.

7800 PICTURE DRIVE • FORTY YEARS OF SERVICE TO THE NATION'S SCHOOLS • MINNEAPOLIS, MINNESOTA 55435 • TELEPHONE (612) 835-3400

R. Bruce Reinecker
Chairman of the Board
and President

Richard P. Erickson
Executive Vice President

ElRoy Nerness
Vice President - Treasurer

Wells J. Wright
Secretary

Steven Subak
Vice President

Dear Fellow Employees:

We present to you with pleasure this booklet which describes the National School Studios, Inc. Employee Stock Ownership Plan. This Plan has been developed after a great deal of study, and we are proud of its design. We hope that the Plan will be highly successful and rewarding in its operation, to the success of our mutual enterprise and the economic security and independence of each Participant.

Our Plan is designed to qualify for preferred tax treatment under Section 401 (a) of the Internal Revenue Code. The Plan documents are available for your inspection and study at the corporate headquarters. If you have any questions, please do not hesitate to ask.

With best wishes,

Sincerely yours,

R. Bruce Reinecker
Chairman of the Board
and President

PROCESSING PLANTS: MINNEAPOLIS, MINNESOTA • DERBY, CONNECTICUT • MUNCIE, INDIANA • KANSAS CITY, MISSOURI

ELROY NERNESS

C hallenges? ElRoy Nerness loved them. The licensed CPA joined Lifetouch in 1977 and masterminded the company's unique employee stock ownership plan. "The ESOP has had double-digit growth every year," he said. "It's been successful because Lifetouch has challenges and opportunities, not problems."

In 1985, Nerness took on a major challenge when NSS bought Pixyfoto, of Cologne, Germany. As senior vice president international, Nerness divided his time between the U.S. and Europe, trying to unravel legal, cultural, and monetary differences. "Here, finances are either black or white," he said. "In Europe, there's gray, too. That was an education for me."

In June 1987, following a routine trip, Nerness suffered a severe heart attack. He retired in 1988, but serves on the Lifetouch board of directors, and currently chairs the ESOP administration committee. Why does Nerness stay involved at Lifetouch? "It's simple," he said. "We've got some of the greatest people around."

"We had to move fast," said Erickson. "There were a lot of details to work out before June 30. If we missed that IRS deadline, we'd have to wait another year." On June 26, 1978, with four days to spare, National School Studios filed with the IRS, making the ESOP effective retroactively to July 1, 1977.

Reinecker's ESOP was unusual in many ways. Unlike most ESOPs, which give partial ownership to employees, NSS's plan would give employees 100 percent ownership, and it would transfer that ownership without any monetary contribution from the employees. To accomplish this, National School Studios established an employee-owned trust which would purchase Reinecker's stock over several years, using funds contributed by NSS from its profits. As Reinecker was NSS's sole owner, he would be, in essence, financing the employees' purchase with his own money over the course of the next five or six years.

With Richard Erickson's leadership, the company continued to prosper under employee ownership, and the sale of Reinecker's stock proceeded on schedule. In 1979, the $26 per share price rose to $30. This increase was a mixed blessing. The owners' stock was now worth more, but the higher price made it more expensive for the trust to purchase Reinecker's remaining shares. What had originally been a five- or six-year buyout now jumped to a 15-year buyout, given the company's rate of growth. "I promised the employees that the company would be in their hands

Staff Photo by Bruce Bisping

R. Bruce Reinecker, owner and president of National School Studios, Inc., Edina.

Owner to 'give away' photo firm

By Jim Fuller
Staff Writer

In 1936, two young men named R. Bruce Reinecker and Eldon Rothgeb started a little business, taking photographs of students in Minnesota schools. That business, now called National School Studios, Inc., prospered over the years, to the point that it will top $30 million in sales this year.

Six years ago Rothgeb died. Reinecker bought his stock under a prearranged payment plan and became sole owner of National School Studios, an Edina-based company that operates school photo programs throughout this country and in West Germany, Puerto Rico and the Virgin Islands.

After his partner's death, Reinecker began to think about what would happen to the company "when I'm spirited away by the gypsies."

How do you dispose of a $30 million business that employs as many as 1,200 people during peak periods of the year?

ElRoy Nerness, vice president and treasurer, said offers to buy the company come in "monthly, almost weekly." But Reinecker has decided to "give it away" at a fraction of its real value.

National School's employees, at least a majority of them, are to become its owners, at no cost to themselves.

Reinecker is given to statements like "No man is an island" and "I've got the greatest bunch of employees in the world."

National School Studios has "been referred to many, many times as a family rather than a company," he said in an interview last week.

Those are cliches used often by corporate executives who are being consciously modest. But Reinecker is putting his money where his mouth is.

National School has set up an employee stock ownership trust (ESOT), which is not in itself unusual. Many companies use such trusts to distribute a certain percentage of their stock to employees. It is a way to compensate key employees for their loyalty and good work and to stimulate more of the same.

What is unusual is that Reinecker has committed himself to turning over complete

National continued on page 22C

More than 40 years after founding National School Studios, Bruce Reinecker's ESOP transferred company ownership to NSS employees.

Throughout the 1970s, Richard Erickson assumed increasing responsibility for NSS's management.

within 10 years and I wasn't about to go back on that promise," Reinecker said in 1986. "Time was slipping away. I asked ElRoy and Dick to find a workable solution for us."

After considering the various alternatives, Nerness and Erickson sat down with Reinecker and discussed his options. "We told him he would get much more money if he continued the yearly stock sale," said Nerness. "If his priority was to get the stock in the hands of the employees immediately, however, the best way to accomplish that was to sell 100 percent of the stock immediately." NSS could make the sale possible by lending the trust enough money to purchase the remaining stock at $30 per share. Because of the financial implications, the two advised Reinecker to think carefully about his decision. But Reinecker's mind was already made up. Greater wealth didn't interest him. "I can only live in one house, I can only drive one car, and I can only wear one suit of clothes at one time," he explained. "What could I do with any more money? There's been enough barking," he concluded. "It's time we treed the coon. I'm going to sell."

NSS became one of the first companies in the nation to be 100 percent employee owned, and Reinecker's generosity was hailed in the business press and in personal letters from top executives at other corporations throughout the country. But the biggest and most meaningful responses came from his employees. "Yours was an act of unselfish

National School Studios, Inc.
EMPLOYEE STOCK OWNERSHIP PLAN
7800 PICTURE DRIVE • MINNEAPOLIS, MINNESOTA 55435 • TELEPHONE (612) 835-3400

generosity and magnificent proportions," wrote Bob Savage, a territory manager in Ohio. (Bob Savage died in 1992. His son, Shawn Savage, manages the Ohio territory.) "It's very difficult to find a way to thank you for your kindness," wrote territory manager Richard Johnson, "because a simple 'thank you' hardly seems enough."

"As a result of Reinecker's generosity," said Nerness, "NSS employees could expect to accrue significant wealth over the course of their employment." In listing some hypothetical dollars-and-cents figures for the *Minneapolis Tribune,* a Menke & Associates consultant calculated that an employee earning $20,000 a year could expect to accumulate $70,000 in 10 years, allowing for a conservative rate of growth. With that in mind, he concluded, many NSS employees could expect to retire with company stock holdings in the six-figure range.

Thanks to Bruce Reinecker, NSS in December 1979 was a significantly different company from the one he had owned with Eldon Rothgeb in 1972. Sales had soared from $14 to $32 million and profits had nearly tripled. The acquisitions of Prestige Portraits and Universal Publications had helped. But Bruce Reinecker, Richard Erickson, and NSS's 1,587 employees had made these impressive numbers a reality. Erickson was justly proud of the company's accomplishments as he looked forward to the challenges of the coming decade. "We were getting organized," he said, "both in management and finances. We were starting to do long-range planning. Now that we had our heads above water, we were looking for the shore and figuring out how to get there."

Bruce Reinecker in 1979.

PROM

SAVE OUR EARTH

PROUD TO BE Me!

Teacher's Guide

WORK HARD

Lifetouch
PORTRAIT STUDIOS INC.

KINDERFOTO INTERNATIONAL
&
JC PENNEY
#1

Lifetouch

Positive Proof!
Exclusive TruView™ Proofing System!

2D
Wednesday/June 8/1994/Star Tribune

Lifetouch may be quiet but it's not little and it's growing under Erickson

To hear Dick Erickson, chairman of Lifetouch Inc., tell it, his is a "quiet little company" that's "doing just fine" in both the sales and earnings departments.

All that proves, however, is that you can take the lad out of the country and dress him up in CEO pinstripes without losing any of the unpretentious gift for understatement he acquired growing up on a farm near Winthrop, Minn.

The fact is, Bloomington-based Lifetouch, the photographer for millions of American students and preschoolers, might be quiet, but it's several hundred million dollars beyond being little.

Consider: Lifetouch revenues in fiscal 1994 ending June 30 will top $350 million — nearly seven times the level when Erickson, 62, became the company's chief executive in 1983.

And while earnings are secret, Erick... allowed as how they have a grati...ng tendency to hit record levels ...st years. The company has 4,000 ...time employees and up to 6,000 ...timers during peak periods.

...ose of you from my generation, ...etouch name might not mean ...lot. But back in the Paleolith... ...hen we were having our zits, ...and goofy grins recorded in ...y the visiting school pho... ...the company was called ...chool Studios.

...nged the name 10 years ...the expanded nature of ...s a result of his first ...CEO. In April 1983 ...nderfoto International ...tography business ...pre-school and

Dick Youngblood

Dick Erickson

offset declining school enrollments.

Erickson, whose brother is WCCO-AM's Roger Erickson, joined National School Studios in Michigan in 1955, driving from town to town as a salesman/photographer. In the early 1960s he was assigned to open a new territory in northwestern Ohio, and in less than 10 years he had turned into a nicely profitable business that was producing more than $350,000 in annual revenues — the equivalent of $1.2 million in today's inflated dollars.

When Rothgeb, the more sales- and marketing-oriented of the partners, died in 1972, Reinecker went looking for someone to complement his own strengths in administration and production and settled on Erickson as

...ch had $45 million ...ime, operated 80 ...cated in shop-...25 others in ...res around the ...ckson has ex-...nnection to ...doubled

Kodak
Photo

Make an appointment

Sesame Street!
only at JCPenney

SUMMER GAMES 1990

THE $\mathcal{V}$ISION

On November 4, 1980, Richard P. Erickson
became president of National School Studios.
Already a strong and successful company,
NSS now entered a decade of monumental
change. In the 1980s, the new generation
Micro-Z camera system revolutionized sales
and production. The acquisition of Kinderfoto,
which doubled the company's size, and a new
name, "Lifetouch," boosted sales and provided
a new corporate identity. Internally, Lifetouch
refined its management structure while carefully nurturing its rich and enduring culture.

1980 to 1994

When Richard Erickson became president of National School Studios, the United States had elected a new leader, Ronald Reagan, who would oversee a rise from economic recession to new heights of prosperity. Computer and telecommunication technology ushered in the information age, allowing Americans to watch rebellion in China, the collapse of Communism, and the dismantling of the Soviet Union as they occurred. Relief at the Cold War's end was short-lived when in Eastern Europe, nation-states entered into bloody ethnic conflicts to settle ancient feuds and territorial claims. In the West, the 1993 North American Free Trade Agreement created new opportunities for businesses in Canada, Mexico, and the United States.

1980 Richard P. Erickson is named president of NSS • U.S. hockey

team wins Olympic Gold • Ronald Reagan is elected president of the

United States **1981** NSS inaugurates formal sales training seminars

• Iran frees 52 Americans held hostage for 444 days •

Prince Charles and Lady Diana Spencer are married in

London **1982** The Micro-Z camera gives NSS a significant

technological edge • Double-digit interest rates push the U.S. into economic

slump **1983** NSS acquires Kinderfoto International, Inc., Reno, Nevada • The

personal computer is *Time* magazine's

"Man of the Year."

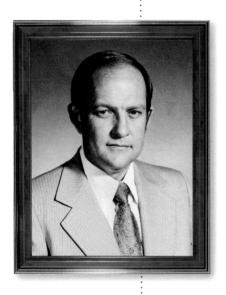

Richard Erickson
was named president
of National School
Studios in November
1980.

Full Speed Ahead

On November 4, 1980, in a sweeping victory, Ronald Reagan was elected the 40th president of the United States. The following day, Bruce Reinecker made this announcement to NSS's employees: "Today our company stands at the pinnacle of success…and the future…is indeed bright. Much of our success is the result of the dedication of purpose, sound business judgment, superb leadership qualities, and plain hard work…of Richard P. Erickson. Therefore, at 5 p.m. yesterday, I appointed Dick Erickson president of National School Studios.

"Congratulations, Mr. President," Reinecker said. "You were elected the same day as another man!"

Ronald Reagan had to rebuild a floundering economy and restore U.S. strength and stature abroad. Erickson, on the other hand, led a robust and profitable company, an industry leader. NSS had quadrupled its size during the previous eight years. It was the largest school photography firm in the country, with 23 percent of the national market. Though Erickson had guided the company to its current position, he preferred to look ahead, not back. "We have the human, financial, and technical resources to continue our current growth and profit patterns for the next 10 years," he told the sales force in 1980. "But we need to think beyond those 10 years. To survive, we must…successfully develop and market new products and invest money wisely for the future."

RICHARD P. ERICKSON

Richard Erickson joined Lifetouch in January 1955 after completing a stint in the army. The young man from Winthrop, Minnesota, was planning to return to the family farm. But his brother, Clif, a National School Studios "picture man," convinced him to come out to Michigan to help photograph kids in Clif's rural territory.

"I didn't know much about cameras," Erickson recalled. He went to Kalamazoo for a day of training, and the next day he was on the road photographing children in one country school after another.

Erickson loved the life of the picture man. "I had a job, money in my pocket, and a new 1955 Ford with a heater and a radio," he said. "I couldn't believe my luck."

But luck had little to do with it. In the years that followed, Erickson's hard work, drive, and skill won him a territory in northwestern Ohio. Twelve years later, that territory was one of the most profitable in the company.

Erickson's outstanding salesmanship and ability to manage money and people caught Bruce Reinecker's eye. When Eldon Rothgeb died in 1972, Reinecker invited Erickson to

Minneapolis as NSS's vice president of sales and marketing. He became executive vice president, then president, then president and CEO, and ultimately, chairman of the Lifetouch board of directors.

Under Richard Erickson's leadership, Lifetouch grew beyond its entrepreneurial foundations to its current status as the industry's corporate giant. In the process, Erickson became, in the words of administrative vice president Ted Koenecke, "the soul of this company."

Vision, goals, and persistence are at the core of Erickson's philosophy. "If you want to be on top of the mountain, you just keep working and moving ahead," he said. "You may stumble and fall back, but eventually you get there." Nearly 40 years after he snapped his first picture, Richard Erickson still relishes the company's challenges and its spirit. "This company has heart," he said. "That's what keeps me working. This is better than any game I ever played in my life. Nothing else even comes close."

"Dick is the spiritual leader, the father of the Lifetouch family."

Paul Harmel

Like his predecessor Bruce Reinecker, Richard Erickson is an avid hunter.

Wicker Chairs and Cameos

One new product, the dual image photo introduced in 1978, was beginning to pay off. This second-sale item sold 540,000 packages in 1980, then 1.6 million packages the following year, adding significantly to NSS's record-breaking $7 million sales increase.

Special item products were also becoming profitable at this time. "Special items were a small operation off in the corner," Gary Goenner recalled. "Then they blossomed. Everybody wanted ID cards, Rolodex cards, annual glossies, and little black-and-white prints. At first, NSS couldn't handle the load. When we told our people that we planned to automate and modernize production, there was near mutiny," Goenner said, "but we did it."

Under the guidance of John Reid, NSS developed two other second-sale products — wicker chair portraits in 1983, and cameo portraits in 1984. These new products added revenues and helped balance work schedules for both sales and plant employees. In 1978, only 20 percent of NSS's business occurred outside the fall season. By 1986, that figure was close to 40 percent.

A New Generation Sales Force

While second-sale products were helping smooth the cyclical nature of the company's business year, Erickson was preparing NSS for even greater success. He and Reid had begun restructuring the sales

In the early 1980s, NSS developed two new second-sale products: cameo and wicker chair portraits.

Lifetouch has always been committed to kids and their families.

organization in 1979, first dividing the country into geographic zones, then adding managerial and production support to each zone. Erickson recognized the need to tackle other sales issues, including management training and territory development. But a survey of the sales force revealed a more critical need: "In 1979, the average age of our territory managers was 57," Erickson recalled. "That meant we were headed for big trouble if we didn't recruit and train a flock of new salespeople and territory managers."

To meet this challenge, NSS created a formal two-week sales training program, replacing the old system of brief workshops and much trial and error. These new training seminars were launched in conjunction with a sales development program designed to improve NSS coverage in areas of low market penetration. "The goal of each sales development area was to become a regular territory," said Jim Haeg, the program's first manager. NSS targeted Dallas, Birmingham, and the east coast of Florida for the first year, and Haeg hired 15 salespeople to develop these areas. The recruits received formal training, and their sales were tracked closely to test the training's effectiveness. They sold 400,000 pictures the first year and doubled that number in the 1984-85 season, bringing in five percent of NSS's total sales.

"That program taught us how to hire and train new salespeople and start new territories," said Haeg. "We then extended the training seminars to existing territories throughout the country." By 1987, NSS was conducting two-week sales training seminars four times a year

1984 A new corporate headquarters in Bloomington,

Minnesota, houses a new corporation, Lifetouch • NSS sales

reach $120 million • Ronald Reagan and George Bush win a second

term, defeating challengers Walter Mondale and Geraldine Ferraro

1985 Lifetouch acquires Pixyfoto of Cologne, West Germany

• David Koentopf joins Lifetouch • Madonna inspires legions of

"Madonna wannabes" **1986** Lifetouch celebrates 50 years in business •

A nuclear power plant disaster occurs at Chernobyl,

USSR • Richard Erickson is appointed chairman of

the Lifetouch board; David Koentopf becomes president.

and offering six-day advanced selling courses, photography training, and management seminars for new territory managers through the company's formal Management Development Program (MDP). MDP graduates have become some of the company's top sales people, proving that training works.

By 1993, the average age of Lifetouch territory managers had dropped to 33 while the number of territories had more than doubled, from 85 (in the late 1970s) to 185. "We now have a young company," said Erickson, "not only in the field but in our production facilities as well. This gives us huge strengths for the future."

The Micro-Z – a New Generation Camera

Like Bruce Reinecker, Richard Erickson strove for technological innovation. He wanted to keep NSS at the forefront of the industry. But the company's rapid growth was taxing its production capabilities. "We were producing nearly 200 million photos a year," Erickson recalled in 1986. "Keeping track of that many units became difficult. We needed a more efficient information system. We had to streamline the photo process without sacrificing quality."

Foreseeing these problems, Erickson had commissioned Tal Hopson in 1978 to devise an entirely new imaging and production system. Hopson now focused his attention on the most important part of the production process — the moment the image is put on the negative. "Production was always trying to compensate for problems on the negative,"

Under the direction of Tal Hopson (not shown), NSS created the revolutionary new Micro-Z camera system in the late 1970s. Representatives of the NSS Sales force on the Micro-Z committee included (left to right): Don Prothero, Bill Porter, Jim Johnson, Clif Erickson, Vern Benmark, Gene Guccione.

Erickson said. "If we could get a uniformly dense negative and correct lighting, and put the proper information on the negative to tell production what to do with it, we would make great leaps forward."

Hopson and his four-member design team first consulted with people in sales and production to determine their needs. The prototype for the camera that eventually became the Micro-Z was unveiled at the July 1980 sales meeting. Most of its features were industry firsts — a double reflex, zoom lens that eliminated camera movement and camera-to-subject measurements; a computerized data recorder that registered all pertinent information and transferred it to the negative in bar code; a 46mm, single-perforation film format (the larger film size incorporated the bar code and name-under identification; single-perforation film helped photographers frame negatives more accurately); a lighting control system sensitive to skin tone; a failure alarm system, for all functions, that eliminated photographer error; and a motorized camera pedestal for easier height adjustments.

Although the camera was a significant advance over the Model 5 then in use, the sales force resisted it. "From day one," Erickson recalled, "there were sparks from every corner." The Micro-Z required training. Photographers had to write in information, use card inserts, and hit a button to provide bar code information. On the production side, the Micro-Z required new, automated printing equipment that allowed

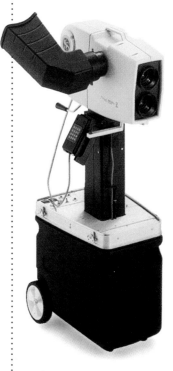

The Micro-Z camera revolutionized NSS's business.

A team of field service technicians keeps the company's Micro-Z cameras in top condition. They include (front, left to right) Tom Myers and Craig Keehr, (back row) Greg Freund, Steve Hughes, Paul Enstad, and Dave Renneberg.

one person to operate four printers instead of one. Production workers feared they would lose their jobs to automation.

What's more, the camera needed refinement before it could fulfill its promise. Between 1980 and 1985, the Micro-Z was redesigned four times to make it more reliable, versatile, and easy to operate. "The improvements made to the original design were nearly as dramatic as the difference between the Model 5 and the Micro-Z," Hopson said. Most important, the camera was now user-friendly. The revamped Micro-Z had a keyboard display that led the photographer through the set-up process and a help file that listed response options.

State-of-the-art production equipment complemented the new cameras. New "Z" printers, designed by Hopson, read the bar code on the negative and automatically printed the correct photo package. Using light pens at their work stations, production workers could trace every order. When the shift to the new cameras and production equipment was complete, no one was happier with the Micro-Z than its champion, Richard Erickson: "It was superb. It reduced plant costs dramatically because of the efficiencies. Waste dropped way down because the negative was correct to begin with. Our error rate declined because the information was on the film. Quality improved because the negatives were consistent. With the Micro-Z we almost doubled our business with the same number of people. And our patent put us years ahead of the competition."

MDP: A SCHOOL FOR MANAGERS

Once upon a time, most Lifetouch territory managers were homegrown. They learned or inherited the business from a father, brother, or in-law. But by the mid-1980s, times were changing, and with them, the complexity of territory management changed as well. Territory managers needed to know much more about technology, management, and finance than their predecessors did.

In July 1987, Lifetouch initiated the Management Development Program (MDP), a comprehensive three-year program designed to develop territory managers. Jan Haeg was among the 12 people selected for the first training class. In 18 months she moved from Minneapolis to St. Louis to San Diego, gaining experience along the way. "I learned photography, the sales side, and operations," she said. "I helped with a Micro-Z training school in Kansas City. With every new experience, I continued to build on my skills."

Haeg returned to Lifetouch NSS headquarters as a human resources field manager. Now, as manager of the MDP program, she oversees the progress of the 30 trainees currently in the program, and recruits new trainees to replace program graduates. So far, 36 MDP graduates have joined the ranks of Lifetouch NSS territory management, representing approximately 25 percent of the total. The program has been judged a success, but MDP is not the only route to management in the field. "No two territory managers are alike," said Haeg. "Every one is different. Our goal is to have a real cross section of experience and background."

New Management Systems

In 1982, National School Studios began to reorganize and expand its management structure in both sales and production. The company appointed a vice president of sales and marketing, a national sales manager, and five zone managers to oversee its 750-member sales force.

On the production side, NSS created a new position — vice president of production — to coordinate research and development, introduce the Micro-Z, oversee budgeting, control costs and waste, and maintain NSS quality. George Kmetz, territory manager and former general manager at the Derby plant and Universal Publications, took on the new job.

NSS salespeople gathered in front of Westminster Church on Nicollet Mall in Minneapolis during the 1982 summer sales meeting.

The company also extended training and information exchanges among plant personnel in its four locations. Led by Jerry Westermann, production and technical employees from Bloomington, Muncie, Derby, and Kansas City organized a three-day annual meeting to learn new production procedures and swap ideas and techniques that would increase productivity.

NSS's efforts to improve sales and increase efficiency paid off. By 1982, sales in the undergraduate division alone were more than $45 million, up from $32 million in 1980. Senior portraits and school annuals added another $10 million in sales, an increase of $3 million over the same period. In 1982, NSS also built and paid for a 22,000-square-foot addition to the Bloomington plant, and for the fifth straight year, made its 15 percent contribution to the ESOP.

Company executives saw 1982 as a successful year, but not as a high point. Instead, it was an indicator of future potential: "We must continue to grow," wrote Bruce Reinecker, board chairman, in a letter to NSS employees. His message to the NSS management team was explicit: "I expect a $100 million company by 1985."

Double Your Pleasure – Kinderfoto

National School Studios had instituted new management structures and internal programs that would ensure strong, steady growth into the future. But to double revenues in three years required something new.

Throughout the 1980s, Lifetouch continued to grow its senior portrait business.

In 1982, NSS set up a corporate development program to oversee company planning, market development, and acquisitions. John Reid, vice president of sales and marketing, assumed the new position, aided by John Flynn, market development manager. Growth by acquisition was their prime goal. "We thought the best fits would be in the preschool photography market and the overseas market," Reid recalled. "Shortly after that, we discovered that Kinderfoto might be amenable to a sale."

NSS doubled its size with the acquisition of Kinderfoto International Inc. In April 1983, NSS chairman Bruce Reinecker met with Kinderfoto founder Stanley Hoke to close the deal.

Stanley Livingston Hoke founded Kinderfoto in 1947 when he set up studios in Fayetteville and Charlotte, North Carolina. By 1982, the company had become the third largest child portrait photography firm in the country, with $45 million in sales generated from 200 permanent studios and 1,400 additional locations served by traveling photographers.

Stanley Hoke was no longer involved in Kinderfoto's day-to-day operations, but he still had strong feelings for his company and his employees' welfare. National School Studios began its discussions with Kinderfoto in November 1982 when Richard Erickson and John Reid visited the company's Reno, Nevada, headquarters. They liked what they saw:

Kinderfoto was approximately the same size as NSS, with a complementary market niche and a commitment to technical excellence. Kinderfoto also had significant market share with high growth potential.

Erickson and Reid, however, had to convince Hoke that NSS would take good care of his company. Erickson appointed Reid executive vice president of NSS to give himself time to pursue the acquisition. ElRoy Nerness and Bruce Reinecker soon joined the team. "Hoke wanted to talk about his employees," Erickson recalled. "How they were trained, how they did their jobs — and about the customers, how important it was to treat them right." NSS's ESOP provided substantial proof that NSS cared about its employees. Furthermore, NSS agreed to a five-year expansion plan for Kinderfoto that would include doubling the size and handling capacity of the Reno plant. Hoke was won over and agreed to the sale.

NSS announced the Kinderfoto acquisition on April 5, 1983, less than a year after Reinecker's $100-million-revenue challenge. Erickson had reached that goal two years ahead of schedule. In the process, National School Studios extended its sphere of influence over the entire portrait photography industry.

Kinderfoto was one of the largest child portrait photography firms in the U.S. when NSS acquired it in 1983.

ROBERT H. TREUCHEL

*R*obert Treuchel was no stranger to large corporations when he joined Lifetouch in 1983. He had spent 16 years in administration at the Marriott Corporation before taking a job at Kinderfoto in 1979. After Lifetouch acquired Kinderfoto, Richard Erickson asked Treuchel to join the newly established headquarters group.

Treuchel organized Lifetouch's first corporate administration department, which included human resources, legal counsel, capital and liability insurance, and employee benefits. Treuchel's role soon evolved into one of adviser and counsel to Erickson. In 1987, after Bruce Reinecker died, he took Reinecker's seat on the board of directors.

As head of administration, Treuchel created systems and an infrastructure to support the rapidly expanding Lifetouch enterprise. The evidence of his work is not in brick and mortar or sales figures, but in smoothly operating systems and employee satisfaction. Treuchel retired from his administrative duties with strong friendships at Lifetouch and a love for the company. "The Lifetouch culture is like a good family, full of loyalty, respect, and honesty," he said.

Blending Companies

Although National School Studios was not a neophyte when it came to acquisitions, having integrated two other companies into the NSS family, the Kinderfoto acquisition presented a new challenge. Kinderfoto was much larger than either Universal or Prestige and had no prior relationship with NSS. Their businesses were similar, yet their marketing styles were poles apart. Kinderfoto was a retailer that relied heavily on advertising and promotions to generate business. National School Studios, Prestige, and Universal were sales-driven companies. In addition, Kinderfoto had recovered only recently from some jolting changes. In 1981, the company had moved its headquarters from Charlotte to Reno and had lost 79 of its 80 administrative employees. The one remaining member of the management team was Robert Treuchel, who had joined the company in 1979 as head of administration and would become a key member of the Lifetouch team.

Having doubled its size, NSS faced another period of change and adjustment. "We were suddenly a $100-million company," said Erickson, who had assumed the role of chief executive officer in February 1983. "And one half of us was 1,500 miles away. What's more, despite its revenues, Kinderfoto was unprofitable. It was an entrepreneurial company that had grown too big. It needed systems, a division of leadership, and people with experience in leadership positions."

The Kinderfoto acquisition made NSS a major force in the entire portrait photography industry.

In 1984, NSS's new headquarters group moved to 7831 Glenroy Road, west of the Bloomington plant.

For Erickson, the Kinderfoto challenge signalled the need to restructure management of the entire organization. "Overnight, we had become four companies and doubled in revenue," Erickson recalled. "We needed to start a headquarters group, separate from the day-to-day activities of the Bloomington plant and dedicated to the growth of the entire company."

The first headquarters group was composed of Bruce Reinecker, chairman of the board; Richard Erickson, president and CEO; ElRoy Nerness, corporate vice president of finance; Richard Palmquist, corporate vice president of production; Robert Treuchel, corporate vice president of administration, and Paul Milne, corporate director of data processing. They moved into the building at 7831 Glenroy Road, just west of the Bloomington plant.

"Dick believed that there should be a corporate umbrella and individual companies," Treuchel recalled. "But there were many questions to be answered. How would the companies be structured? What would be the working relationships among them? What part would be corporate? What would be a division, or a subsidiary?" The headquarters group decided to give each division autonomy around its customers and markets. The headquarters group would link and coordinate sales and marketing, administration, production, and communications for each division, promote cooperation among divisions, and develop the company's overall strategy.

"We wanted a lean, efficient headquarters group," said Erickson. "We kept it lean by keeping the divisions relatively independent and by putting strong managers in charge of them." With this structure, NSS had formulated a management framework that would continue into the mid-1990s.

A New Name

The work of the headquarters group revealed another important company need — a single name to identify the entire corporation. National School Studios, Prestige Portraits, Universal Publications, and Kinderfoto International all had separate identities that few people outside the company linked together. "We have become one company with the ability to photograph everyone in the United States — all 240 million people," wrote Richard Erickson in a 1984 letter to employees. "But very few people know all our abilities and strengths. We need a name that will help people recognize us as THE company to turn to for great photographs at great values."

In January 1984, Richard Erickson and Bruce Reinecker announced plans to develop a new corporate identity and hired Lippincott and Margulies, Inc., of New York, to help. Over the next several months, the firm generated hundreds of names, which NSS officials and the legal department whittled down to seven. "We didn't want a name that was

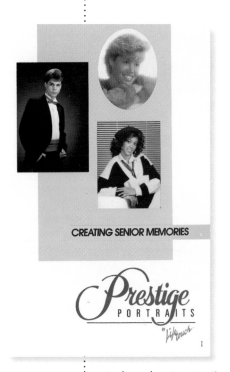

CREATING SENIOR MEMORIES

Prestige PORTRAITS

In the early 1980s, Prestige Portraits was one of four operating companies in the NSS family.

On August 1, 1984, NSS changed its name to Lifetouch. Richard Erickson announced the new name to employees at the summer sales meeting in Minneapolis.

too explicit. We wanted room to grow," Erickson recalled. "That eliminated the word 'photo'. The name also had to suggest the preservation of memories, but we didn't want to use 'memory.' That would have made us sound old-fashioned."

On August 1, 1984, after eight months of deliberation, Richard Erickson announced the company's new name at a festive ceremony that included fireworks, noisemakers, and the release of 3,000 balloons. "We are in the business of preserving memories and touching the lives of people," he said. "We need a name that reflects what we do and how we affect people's lives. I am proud to announce the new name of our company is Lifetouch."

At the same time, each subsidiary was renamed: National School Studios became Lifetouch National School Studios, Kinderfoto became Lifetouch Portrait Studios, Prestige Portraits became Lifetouch Senior Portraits, and Universal Publications became Lifetouch Publishing. Erickson also unveiled the new corporate logo, the word Lifetouch in script. "The logo reinforces our commitment to excellence," he said. "It looks like we're signing our work."

German Pixy

In February 1985, Lifetouch launched a new international division with the acquisition of Pixyfoto GmbH, headquartered in Cologne, West Germany. Like Lifetouch Portrait Studios (Kinderfoto), Pixyfoto operated out of department stores and malls in Germany, France, Holland, and

England. After more than 20 years in business, Pixyfoto's sales volume was $11 million. Stanley Hoke had owned Pixyfoto. In 1979 he sold the company to Hal Melahn, who expressed an interest in selling Pixyfoto when Erickson visited in October 1984. Despite the differences in culture, language, and currency, the acquisition seemed a good fit. Besides, Erickson was not one to shrink from a challenge.

In January 1985, Senior Vice President of Finance ElRoy Nerness flew to Germany, where despite jet lag and language problems, he plunged into a two-week crash course in German business practices. On February 5, 1985, the sale was completed. "The document that closed the million-dollar deal was one page," said Nerness, "German on the left and English on the right." It was a stark example of the differences between U.S. laws and German federal code, differences that would later prove to be insurmountable.

After Pixyfoto's acquisition, ElRoy Nerness led Lifetouch's new international division, assuming the titles of senior vice president international and treasurer, and dividing his time between corporate headquarters in Bloomington and Cologne, Germany. There, he managed 700 people working in 143 fixed and 44 traveling studios.

In January 1985, while Bruce Reinecker (center) and Richard Erickson (right) guided the company at home, ElRoy Nerness (left) took over the company's new international division.

The Lifetouch name brought unity to a multifaceted corporation.

"We acquired it at the right price, but Pixyfoto's potential was difficult to develop," Nerness recalled. The company struggled with currency restrictions in France and with privacy laws that prohibited telemarketing in other countries. Then the deutsche mark rose in value against the dollar and Pixyfoto became a very expensive operation. Meanwhile, changes at home were taking center stage.

Top Management Restructuring

By 1986, 50 years after the company's founding, Chairman of the Board Bruce Reinecker had fulfilled his every dream for the company and had achieved every personal goal he had set for himself. With one exception — he had worked 46 years past his 30th birthday, his original retirement goal. Even in 1986, Reinecker kept his hand on the helm, assuming the position of chairman emeritus to offer guidance and counsel to the organization. He said at the time, "I hope they keep me on until I have a daisy in my hand."

After more than three decades at Lifetouch, nearly half in key leadership roles, Richard Erickson became chairman of the board as well as chief executive officer in 1986. Executive Vice President David Koentopf, who had joined Lifetouch a year earlier, was named president and chief operating officer. Koentopf initiated the company's first formal strategic planning process. Another key management change followed when Paul Harmel, who was named vice president of finance in 1984, became vice president of operations at Lifetouch NSS.

WOMEN AT LIFETOUCH

*F*lexibility and seasonal work schedules once held the greatest appeal to women at Lifetouch. But today's high-growth, team-oriented company atmosphere is drawing career-oriented women into sales and management ranks as well as production and administration.

Since 1977, Judy Benjamin has moved from money counter and backup receptionist at Minneapolis headquarters to territory manager in Arizona. In 13 years, she grew her territory from 60,000 to 500,000 photographs a year. Even though her territory has been split in two, she still has her hands full managing a staff of 35 professionals who operate 37 Micro-Z cameras a day and shoot 250,000 photographs a season.

Former Prestige Portrait sales manager Debbie DiGiacomo joined Lifetouch in 1983. She crisscrossed the country developing new markets before assuming the role of director of business development in 1992. In the past two years, she has managed the acquisition of nearly 20 companies in the U.S., Canada, and Mexico. In July 1994, DiGiacomo will return to sales management

Judy Benjamin (above),
Debbie DiGiacomo (below).

to oversee four regional managers and 60 territories in the western United States.

Women are also active in developing new products and marketing strategies. Diane L. Greenberg, Lifetouch Portrait Studios director of creative and product development, is exploring the use of digital imagery and PhotoCD™ technology to expand the division's in-house creative capabilities. She's also part of a management team that develops and launches new products. Lifetouch Senior Portraits marketing manager Nancy Dahl is responsible for designing the products, promotions, advertising, and pricing for eight senior market territories east of the Mississippi. At the same time, she tracks technologies that offer new opportunities for Lifetouch products. Melinda Sorenson, a director of marketing for Lifetouch Portrait Studios, seeks new products and advertising to grow the studio portrait business throughout the United States.

Have opportunities changed for women at Lifetouch? "I never felt that women weren't able to progress," said DiGiacomo. "The opportunities have been there for those willing to work hard, communicate well, and do the job."

Diane L. Greenberg (above, right), Nancy Dahl (below), Melinda Sorenson (right).

In the mid-1980s, Lifetouch NSS created peel-and-stick Picture Pals.

Improving From Within

Under its evolving leadership, Lifetouch continued to develop new products, new sales techniques, and new production methods that boosted sales and improved efficiency. Focusing their attention on marketing strategies, Lifetouch Publishing and Lifetouch Senior Portraits created market development groups. Lifetouch Portrait Studios added family portraits to its product line; Lifetouch NSS introduced Picture Pals and child I.D. kits and improved picture quality at its Bloomington and Derby plants with Photogard, a coating process that protects negatives.

At the same time, Lifetouch corporation was gaining strength by concentrating its divisional management in Bloomington. In July 1985, Lifetouch Portrait Studios had moved its corporate headquarters from Nevada to Minnesota. "We…[are] carrying out our strategy," Richard Erickson said, "of pulling…the separate corporate strands [of] our company into one cohesive organization that is…moving forward in the same direction at the same time." (Consolidation would continue in 1988, when Lifetouch Senior Portraits would move its headquarters from Muncie to Bloomington.)

Fifty years after its founding, Lifetouch consisted of five divisional companies — National School Studios, Portrait Studios, Publishing, Senior Portraits, and the International Division. Together, they generated annual sales of $150 million and were owned by an ESOP appraised at $91 a share.

Bruce and Vye Reinecker took a walk in Reinecker Park, adjacent to Lifetouch NSS, following the park's dedication in the fall of 1984.

The Torch is Passed

On October 4, 1987, Lifetouch founder R. Bruce Reinecker died in his sleep. He was 77 years old. Only the day before, he and Richard Erickson had breakfast at 4 a.m., then headed to the marsh for some duck hunting, a sport he loved.

Eulogizing his friend, Erickson spoke of Reinecker's zest for life and the qualities he had imparted to his company: "He left a legacy that is a guide for us in the future — fairness in our dealings with people, integrity, honesty, and a can-do, will-do attitude." In a special memorial publication, people in the company recounted Reinecker's many acts of kindness, generosity, and friendship, and his love for the company. "Everything he had done was directed toward building a staff that could take over, and that's exactly what happened," said Steve Subak.

Lifetouch continued to grow following Reinecker's death. In July 1989, the company acquired Enterprise School Photos, Inc., a school picture and yearbook wholesaler based in Tulsa, Oklahoma. The acquisition gave Lifetouch a new market in photo finishing for independent portrait studios. Fred Bosworth, former national sales manager of Lifetouch NSS, was named executive vice president and chief operating officer of the wholesale operation.

Lifetouch's next acquisition took place in January 1990 with the purchase of Max Ward-Delmar, the leading supplier of undergraduate and senior portrait services in North Carolina, Virginia, Delaware, and

1987 Bruce Reinecker dies in Minneapolis  • The New York stock market plummets 508 points, the worst one-day crash in financial history • Paul Harmel is named vice president and chief operating officer for Lifetouch NSS. **1988** Lifetouch acquires Video Creations of St. Paul, Minnesota **1989** Lifetouch acquires Enterprise School Photos, Inc., of Tulsa, Oklahoma • George Bush becomes the 41st president  of the United States • The Berlin Wall is opened **1990** Lifetouch acquires Max Ward-Delmar, Chesapeake, Virginia • Nelson Mandela, symbol of the struggle for equality in South Africa, is freed after 27 years in prison • John Goodrich is named vice president and chief operating officer for Lifetouch Portrait Studios.

The acquisition of Max Ward-Delmar gave Lifetouch entry into the preschool portrait market.

Maryland. The acquisition provided Lifetouch with a 60,000-square-foot office and laboratory facility in Chesapeake, Virginia.

The acquisition also gave Lifetouch an entree into a new market niche — preschool photography — through Portrait Industries Corporation (PIC), a Max Ward-Delmar division. As the nation's leading supplier of portrait packages to preschool day care centers, PIC served day care centers in 46 states and operated 20 fixed portrait studios in Montgomery Ward stores in Maryland and Virginia. To aid in the transition, Max Ward-Delmar's president, Jim Saine, remained with Lifetouch.

Poised for the Future

In March 1991, Lifetouch's acquisitions and growth prompted another reorganization and expansion effort. Lifetouch created the School Group, a division with four parts: Lifetouch National School Studios, Lifetouch Senior Portraits, Lifetouch Publishing, and Lifetouch Video Creations (a high school video yearbook company acquired in 1988).

Lifetouch Portrait Studios became a separate 2,800-employee retail division, specializing in studio photography in 430 JC Penney department stores, 500 traveling studios serving rural JC Penney locations, and 80 Kinderfoto studios in major malls on the East and West coasts. John Goodrich, who joined Lifetouch in 1986 as vice president for finance, had been chosen to lead Lifetouch Portrait Studios in 1990.

Enterprise School Photos, Inc., headquartered in Tulsa, Oklahoma, became the company's wholesale division, specializing in photo finishing for independent portrait studios throughout the country. Lifetouch's fourth division, PIC Inc., headquartered in Mobile, Alabama, was set up to market photography at day care centers nationwide.

A New Executive Committee

In December 1992, Richard Erickson improved the management of the burgeoning organization by creating a new executive committee. It included the chairman, president, three corporate officers, and two line officers. The committee met every other month to discuss company issues, and share problems and solutions. "This is a small, closely knit group," said committee member John Goodrich, chief operating officer of Portrait Studios. "We have open communication, with no big egos and a lot of brain power. But the best thing about it is the camaraderie and the heart. People's values and feelings for the company are all the same."

Soul Searching

"Our success over the last 10 years has been phenomenal," said Mark Kilchenman, senior executive vice president and chief operating officer of the School Group. "It has changed the dynamics of this company in many ways. At the same time we have this family tradition. Holding

The 1991 corporate reorganization made Lifetouch Portrait Studios a separate retail division, specializing in studio photography.

on to that tradition and the company's underlying values are the keys to perpetuating our unique culture." Richard Erickson concurs, "Lifetouch has a heart, a home, security, growth, talent. Anybody who is here for a short time gets to feel that."

The culture at Lifetouch is a special blend of seemingly incongruous elements — young and dynamic, yet stable and rooted in family values, informal and fun-loving, yet disciplined, with everyone striving for excellence. Even with a formal management structure, the company strives for informality, with little hierarchy. "I've spent 29 years with Lifetouch and it's never seemed like a job," said Jim Haeg. "For most of us this is a way of life." Many Lifetouch people are friends both on and off the job. An atmosphere of respect for individual effort permeates the company.

What makes the culture so strong? "People have asked me if the ESOP was the magic bullet," said Erickson. "And I say no, an ESOP won't make a bad company good. And it's not going to make leadership obsolete, either. But if you have a good company with good, dedicated people who work for a common cause, the results are going to be positive."

Lifetouch people work very hard. "The time and effort, and energy expended is really huge," said Haeg. "But it's not a job. It's more like getting together with friends. We know we can succeed. We can do whatever we want to do. That's a feeling you can't touch or bottle. But you can perpetuate it."

Members of Richard Johnson's "C" Territory gathered in September 1991.

LIFETOUCH COMMITMENT TO EDUCATION

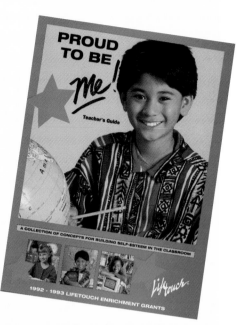

or Lifetouch, involvement in education goes far beyond the business of school photography. The company provides schools throughout the country with programs and creative educational materials that enhance the quality of life and learning for children.

In recent years, the Lifetouch Enrichment Grant Program has supported the efforts of schools to promote diversity and multiculturalism, environmental awareness and protection, community service and volunteerism, and self-esteem building. Through these subjects, the program helps instill strong values while recognizing the creative efforts of outstanding teachers.

The company donates $100,000 each year to elementary and secondary schools nationwide to support special curriculum development in these areas. For example, in the 1992-93 school year, nearly 4,000 teachers from across North America submitted ideas for improving self-esteem in the classroom. A Lifetouch panel of educators selected 280 winners,

BUILDING PROJECT

Helping a Local Homeless Shelter: Constructing a Playground

GOALS

This activity will encourage students to:
- Realize the importance of community service
- Learn skills such as planning and budgeting
- Give children with very little an opportunity for recreation

DESCRIPTION

Once it has been determined that a local homeless shelter has outdoor space for a playground, students work with the shelter's director, teachers and community leaders to plan and design it. Students also plan and participate in fund-raising activities for necessary materials and equipment.

Once all has been purchased for the playground, students assist community leaders and the shelter's director in constructing the playground. People staying in the shelter might volunteer as well. If the shelter is in an unsafe area, community members and students may consider fencing the playground.

Building a playground allows students to realize the importance of helping others and gives them a feeling of self-worth.

Submitted by
John Naeher, Christian Heritage School, Trumbull, Connecticut

Students plan, construct and raise money for a playground to be used by families staying at the local homeless shelter.

14

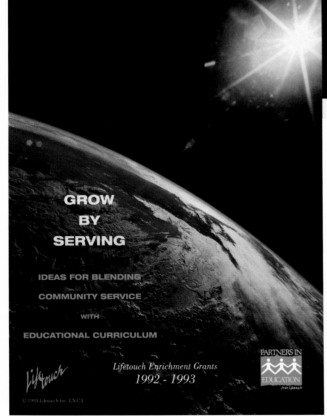

GROW
BY
SERVING

IDEAS FOR BLENDING

COMMUNITY SERVICE

WITH

EDUCATIONAL CURRICULUM

Lifetouch Enrichment Grants
1992 - 1993

PARTNERS IN
EDUCATION
from Lifetouch

who received grants of $250 to $1,000 each to support their curriculum plans. Award-winning ideas were compiled in a teacher's guide, which was distributed to all program participants.

Partners in Education, another Lifetouch program, provides schools with complimentary recognition items to encourage and reward student achievement. Up to 30 items, including bookmarks, birthday cards, and certificates of achievement, are used by schools to reinforce students' achievement efforts. "Partners in Education differentiates us from our competition," said Mark Kilchenman. "But more important, it is an opportunity to give something back to schools."

Management Transition

In 1992, President and Chief Executive Officer David Koentopf left the company and board chairman Richard Erickson reassumed his role as chief executive officer. "Dave was a highly disciplined person who brought us processes that put things in order," Erickson reflected. Erickson resumed the strategic planning process initiated by Koentopf in the late 1980s. On December 2, 1992, Erickson told the executive committee, "We've got many signals about what we're going to do in the future and what our businesses are going to be." He then charged the committee members with two responsibilities: to articulate the company's mission and to organize an operating structure for the individual companies. "They went off by themselves and worked for seven days," Erickson recalled.

Lifetouch was in the business of imaging, the group decided. The market for imaging was estimated at $2.5 billion — plenty of room to grow for Lifetouch. "We're very good at taking photographs in mass volume in a professional way," said Paul Harmel. "That's really our business." To which Erickson responded, "And we're doing a 'measly' $350 million's worth. We have only 12 to 14 percent of the market — and we haven't left the borders of the U.S."

A few weeks later, Erickson named Paul Harmel president and chief operating officer of Lifetouch, Inc. and its subsidiaries. Harmel, who had 16 years' experience at Lifetouch, had been chief operating officer of Lifetouch NSS since 1987.

In 1991, members of the Lifetouch Senior Portraits team were recognized with a performance award at the winter sales meeting.

Lifetouch supports education through annual grants and curriculum materials.

Like Erickson, Harmel personifies the Lifetouch culture. "One of my biggest jobs is to be a good steward," he said. "I want to make sure Lifetouch doesn't lose its magic."

"We're very fortunate," said Ted Koenecke, vice president of administration. "We had Eldy and Bruce — they started it. We had Dick who perpetuated it and made it grow. And now we've got continuity in leadership and a strong focus that will help us maintain our culture while continuing to move forward. Paul Harmel brings to the job vision, integrity, and the interest of the employees, ensuring a strong future for Lifetouch."

Innovation Leads

Through the 1980s and 1990s, Lifetouch continued to lead the industry in technological development. Despite early fears, increasing automation did not cut jobs. Instead, increased sales expanded the need for production, and technological advances placed new demands on the production staff. In 1992 and 1993, production employees were trained in statistical process control, a system designed to further cut costs, increase efficiencies, and improve picture quality.

Next, Lifetouch has taken on digital imaging, generally recognized as the business's next revolution. Digital imaging does not use film. It breaks the subject image into pixels, individual bits of information stored on a computer. Each 35mm frame contains 25 million pixels and demands sizable chunks of computer

memory. "Multiply that one photo by 500 youngsters in one school, and then multiply that by the thousands of schools we photograph every year," said Erickson. "Memory requirements are stupendous."

By 1994, the company had come a long way but had not completely mastered digital technology. "It has been a challenge and a half," said Gary Goenner, vice president for production. "We have computer experts, printing experts, and pre-press experts, but there's nobody yet who can preside over the whole puzzle."

Lifetouch is continually refining and improving its digital imaging system for color photography. Thirty territories are equipped with prototype digital programs called Vision.™ In Bloomington, Lifetouch computer experts are developing a system in which computers in the field can talk directly to the production facility by modem.

Digital technology promises to open up new products and markets for Lifetouch. "Schools can receive a CD with all the pictures on it, an electronic Rolodex," said Erickson. "The computer will search for a picture, access it, and print it out, or send it over a phone line."

Yet the opportunities provided by digital technology come at a price. High research and development costs raise the stakes for everyone in the industry. "There will be bigger losers and bigger winners in the future because of the investment," said Erickson. "We take 25 million negatives a year. If you're going to digitize them, you'd better be very fast, very inexpensive, and very good. But that's always been our goal — to create a good quality portrait inexpensively."

Today, Lifetouch photographs millions of school children throughout the U.S.

PAUL HARMEL

*I*n basketball and business, Lifetouch President Paul Harmel has proven himself a great team player. Harmel was named South Dakota's most valuable high school basketball player in 1968 after leading his small-town team to the state championship. In college, he chose business over a coaching career and earned a degree in accounting. After graduation, he joined a Minneapolis CPA firm.

In 1977, a friend suggested that Harmel interview for the controller position at NSS. After meeting with Richard Erickson, he decided NSS was right for him. "I felt right away there was something special about the company," he said. "It was unique."

At NSS, Harmel upgraded the existing financial structure with department budgets and forecasts, a first for the company. He worked closely with people in sales, marketing, and production using his abilities in financial analysis to help improve growth and profitability.

Throughout the 1980s, Harmel helped manage the company's explosive growth and the changes that accompanied it. As controller, he was responsible for Kinderfoto's financial integration with NSS. He administered the company's ESOP during its early years, served as an original member of the company's executive committee, and was on the four-member team that chose the new Lifetouch name.

When Lifetouch created a new management structure in 1984 by forming separate operating companies under the corporate umbrella, Harmel began his rise through Lifetouch NSS. He was named vice president of finance, then vice president of operations, and then executive vice president and chief operating officer. In December 1992, Harmel was named president of Lifetouch Inc.

While he is mindful of the challenges that lie ahead, Harmel is committed to preserving the values and traditions of the company's past. "I've always said that one of my biggest responsibilities is to be a good steward of the Lifetouch culture," said Harmel. "That means making sure it doesn't lose its magic."

"Paul Harmel brings to the job vision, integrity, and the interest of the employees, ensuring a strong future for Lifetouch."

Ted Koenecke

Lifetouch's technological superiority helps it achieve the highest levels of photographic quality.

Planning the Future

If he were disposed to looking backward, Richard Erickson would view his Lifetouch accomplishments with satisfaction. "Our two main strategies — to more than double our revenues and territories and to hire more people — were accomplished. We became the low-cost, high-quality producer with the Micro-Z. Our market share grew dramatically. In 1978, we had sales of about $23 million. In fiscal 1993-94, we will have sales of $350 million. What has happened in the last five years started in 1977, 1978, 1979. Though we made mistakes and false starts, we always knew what our goal was. If you want to get on top of the mountain, you have to keep working on it until you get there."

Facing 2000 to 2099

But Richard Erickson is now looking to the next century. "What's going to happen in this industry, in our company? What are the possibilities? That's the world I live in," he said. "I need to be drawing a road map for Lifetouch to follow. If you don't have a road map, you may be going down the road, but you have no clue where you're going to wind up. You're always in strange territory."

1991 The United States and its allies unleash Operation Desert Storm against Iraq • Clarence Thomas joins the U.S. Supreme Court despite accusations of sexual harassment by law professor Anita Hill **1992** Arkansas Governor Bill Clinton defeats incumbent George Bush to become president of the United States • Paul Harmel is named Lifetouch president and chief operating officer • Mark Kilchenman is named senior executive vice president and chief operating officer for Lifetouch NSS. **1993** The Serbian siege of Bosnia's capital, Sarajevo, begins its second year **1994** Nelson Mandela is elected president of South Africa • Lifetouch sales hit $350 million as the company enters new international markets.

The sculpture *Familia,* by Paul Granlund, symbolizes Lifetouch's commitment to families.

Erickson draws his inspiration from the dedication and personal commitment of Lifetouch people, their high ethical standards, and their willingness to take risks. "It all goes back to heart," he said. "We have the company organized for the future, and we've got bright, talented, committed, and dedicated people."

By 1994, Lifetouch operated production facilities in nine locations — Bloomington, Minnesota; Derby, Connecticut; Muncie, Indiana; Kansas City, Missouri; Tulsa, Oklahoma; Reno, Nevada; Chico, California; Chesapeake, Virginia; and Love's Park, Illinois. Lifetouch was present in every state in the country, had operations in Canada and Puerto Rico, and, in late 1993, took its first steps into Mexico. The company is a giant in its industry, with divisions covering multiple markets.

Looking ahead, Richard Erickson is alert to unforeseen obstacles. "Who is our competitor that we don't know about?" he wonders. "Will there be an industry out there that will blindside us?"

As Lifetouch moves forward with its technological advances, its vision for the future, and its deeply felt culture, it is prepared for marvels not yet dreamed. And no doubt, the people of Lifetouch will be creating them.

ACKNOWLEDGEMENTS

We want to thank everyone who participated in the creation of this book. We particularly want to thank Jan Youngdahl, whose corporate memory has been invaluable in the reconstruction of recent decades. In addition to her memory of events and people, Jan contributed to the book by finding many of the items pictured or reproduced in its pages.

The following individuals contributed through interviews or by helping locate materials for the book:

Judy Benjamin
Nancy Dahl
Bill DeCoursey
Ernie Denogeon
Debbie DiGiacomo
Roberta Elliott
Clif Erickson
Richard Erickson
John Goodrich
Tina Goskey
Fred Gowan

Gary Goenner
Diane Greenberg
Jan Haeg
Jim Haeg
Paul Harmel
Vicki Hodapp
Mark Kilchenman
Verla Kolberg
Jaci Larson
ElRoy Nerness
Margaret Newman

Marte Palm
Richard Palmquist
Jeff Reid
John Reid
Dianne Schueller
Ether Searle
Melinda Sorenson
Steve Subak
Bob Treuchel
Peggy Wheelock
Dean Wilson

Ted L. Koenecke

Ted L. Koenecke
Corporate Vice President of Administration

BOARD OF DIRECTORS

Richard P. Erickson
Paul Harmel
Robert H. Treuchel

Richard A. Hassel
John Reid
ElRoy Nerness

Donald Goldfus
Phillip Samper
Robert Larson

INDEX